CiA Revision Series

ECDL®/ICDL® Advanced AM3 Word Processing

using Microsoft® Word

Dawn Harvey

Published by:

CiA Training Ltd
Business & Innovation Centre
Sunderland Enterprise Park
Sunderland SR5 2TH
United Kingdom

Tel: +44 (0) 191 549 5002
Fax: +44 (0) 191 549 9005

info@ciatraining.co.uk
www.ciatraining.co.uk

ISBN 1-86005-338-6

Release RS01v1

First published 2005

Approved Courseware Advanced Syllabus AM 3 Version 1.0

CiA Training's **Revision Exercises** for **Advanced ECDL** contain a collection of revision exercises to provide support for students. They are designed to reinforce the understanding of the skills and techniques which have been developed whilst working through CiA Training's ***AM3 - Word Processing*** book.

The exercises contained within this publication are not ECDL tests. To locate your nearest ECDL test centre please go to the ECDL Foundation website at ***www.ecdl.com****.*

Advanced Word Processing - The revision exercises cover the following topics, grouped into sections:

- Text Editing
- Paragraph Editing
- Advanced Printing
- Document Layout
- Tables
- Text Boxes
- Graphics & Drawings
- Referencing
- Templates
- Collaborative Editing
- Document Security
- Master Documents
- Field Codes and Forms
- Mail Merge
- Working with Spreadsheets
- Macros

A minimum of two revision exercises is included for each section. There are also general exercises, which cover techniques from any section of this guide. Answers are provided at the end of the guide wherever appropriate.

The Revision Exercises are suitable for:

- Any individual wishing to practise advanced features of this application. The user completes the exercises as required. Knowledge of *Word* is assumed, gained for example from working through the corresponding ***AM3 - Word Processing*** book produced by **CiA**.

- Tutor led groups as reinforcement material. They can be used as and when necessary.

Aims and Objectives

To provide the knowledge and techniques necessary to be able to successfully tackle the features of an advanced word processing application. After completing the exercises the user will have experience in the following areas:

- Applying advanced text and paragraph editing
- Creating and modifying templates
- Tracking changes and working with comments
- Working with sections and columns
- Creating tables of contents, indexes, footnotes and endnotes
- Using field codes, forms and document protection
- Modifying graphics and applying captions
- Editing mail merge documents
- Working with Macros
- Using advanced printing features

Requirements

These revision exercises were created for *Microsoft Word*. They assume that the computer is already switched on, that a printer and mouse are attached and that the necessary programs have been fully and correctly installed on your computer. However, in *Word,* some features are not installed initially and a prompt to insert the *Office* CD may appear when these features are accessed.

Downloading the Data Files

The data associated with these exercises must be downloaded from our website: ***www.ciatraining.co.uk/data_files***. Follow the on screen instructions to download the data files.

By default, the data files will be downloaded to **My Documents\CIA DATA FILES\Advanced ECDL Revision Series\AM3 Word Processing**. The data required to complete the exercises is in the **Word Processing Data** folder and worked solutions for every exercise can be found in the **Word Processing Solutions** folder.

If you prefer, the data can be supplied on CD at an additional cost. Contact the Sales team at ***info@ciatraining.co.uk***.

Notation Used Throughout This Guide

- All key presses are included within < > e.g. <Enter>
- Menu selections are displayed, e.g. File | Open
- The guide is split into individual exercises. Each exercise consists of a sequential number of steps

Recommendations

- Read the whole of each exercise before starting to work through it. This ensures understanding of the topic and prevents unnecessary mistakes.
- It is assumed that the language selected is English (UK). If this is not the case select **Tools | Language**, select English (UK) and then the Default button.
- Some fonts used in this guide may not be available on all computers. If this is the case, select an alternative.
- Additional information and support for CiA products can be found at: www.ciasupport.co.uk, e-mail: contact@ciasupport.co.uk

The following revision exercises are divided into sections, each targeted at specific elements of the Advanced ECDL syllabus. The individual sections are an exact match for the sections in the ECDL Advanced Training Guides from CiA Training, making the guides an ideal reference source for anyone working through these exercises.

Text Editing

These exercises include topics taken from the following list: Applying text effects, animating text, using **AutoCorrect** and **AutoFormat**, creating **AutoText**, changing text flow and wrap, changing text orientation, applying text design features (**WordArt**).

Exercise 1

1. Open the document **Chinese New Year**.

2. Delete the title and replace it with **WordArt**, using the following style if available: (first style on the third row).

3. The text should read **Chinese New Year**. Make sure the **WordArt** layout is 'floating' and move the text to a suitable position at the top centre of page 1.

4. Change the skew of the graphical text, so that it leans to the right.

5. Animate the word **Fireworks** in the last sentence of paragraph 2 on page **1**, to represent the fireworks.

6. Increase the size of all the underlined paragraph headings to **12pt** and change the colour to orange. Use the **Format Painter** to apply the same formatting to the other titles.

Chinese New Year

Overview

The Chinese New Year falls on a different date each year, because the Chinese calendar combines solar and lunar movements. A new moon on the first day of New Year marks the start of Chinese New Year and it ends 15 days later with the full moon. To synchronise the lunar and solar cycles, the Chinese add an extra month every few years.

The highlights of the festivities are New Year's Eve and New Year's Day, when family is of the utmost importance. This includes the ancestors who have died, but who still command great respect, as they have built the foundations of the family. On New Year's Eve the family holds a banquet for the ancestors; the feast represents family unity. Fireworks are set off to see out the old year and all doors and windows in the house must be opened to let it out.

7. Use the same function to apply an emboss effect to these headings.

8. In the paragraph about **Rituals** only, italicise all text beneath the first sentence.

9. On page 2, change the text wrapping so that text is wrapped **square** to the left of the bamboo graphic.

10. At the bottom of page 2, draw a text box. If necessary press <**Esc**> immediately to remove the drawing canvas.

11. Enter the text **Edited by** and then your name.

12. Change the font to **Arial 10pt bold**. Change the direction of the text so that it reads vertically from bottom to top.

13. Ensure there is only a single line of text and the frame fits it neatly.

14. Move the text box to the left of the final item, **The Home**, ensuring the bottom of the text box is level with the last line of text.

15. Save the document as **Chinese New Year2** and close it.

Exercise 2

1. Open the document **Topperville Hall**.

2. Create an entry that will automatically replace the initials **JM** with **Jeremy Montague** as you type.

3. At the end of the document, type the following paragraph to test the automatic text:

   Plans for the Future

   JM plans to restore the west wing of the hall, which was partially destroyed by fire in 2003. Once complete, this area will house the family art collection and will be known as the JM Gallery.

4. Create an automatic text entry that inserts the phrase **For further information, contact** and name the entry **Info**.

5. Insert this automatic text at the end of the document, followed by the names and telephone numbers indicated:

The House	**Clara McTavish 0121 123456**
The Gardens	**Joseph Spade 0121 123457**
Pets' Corner	**Bunny Tompkins 0121 123458**
Gift Shop	**Sunita Singh 0121 123459**
Tea Room	**Betty Scone 0121 123455**

6. Delete the **AutoText** entries for **JM** and **Info**.

7. Save the document as **Topperville Hall2** and close it.

8. Open the document **Marine Zoology**.

9. Apply **General Document** automatic formatting to this document.

10. Notice that the automatic formatting has not been applied to the **Diet** heading. You should always check documents carefully after using this feature. Use the format painter to copy the formatting of the previous heading to the unformatted one.

11. Use the **Format | Font** command to apply a text effect to the first item of text currently in bold, which will make it all capital letters. After doing this, use the format painter to apply the formatting to the remaining bold text.

12. Save the document as **Marine Zoology2** and close it.

Paragraph Editing

These revision exercises include topics taken from the following list: shading paragraphs, adding borders to paragraphs, setting widow and orphan controls, creating and modifying styles and applying outline levels to styles.

Exercise 3

1. Open the document **Republic**.

2. Create the following styles:

   First Title Times New Roman, 16pt, centred, space after 18pt, level 1.

   Next Title Times New Roman, 12pt, bold, left aligned, space after 12pt, level 2.

   Mainbody Garamond, 12pt, justified, space after 6pt.

3. Activate the **Show/Hide** feature and delete any blank lines used to add space between paragraphs.

4. Apply the **First Title** style to the first line of text, **The End of the Roman Republic**.

5. Apply the **Next Title** style to the headings **Dictatorship**, **Power Struggle** and **Emperor**.

6. Apply the **Mainbody** style to the rest of the text.

7. Print the document.

8. Modify the **First Title** style to be dark blue.

9. In **Outline View**, display only levels 1 and 2 and print the document.

10. Turn off the **Show/Hide** feature. Save the file as **Republic Outline** and close it.

Exercise 4

1. Open the document **Chinese New Year**.

2. Amend the **Body Text** style to have **1½** line spacing.

3. Ensure a single line of text will never be left alone at the top or bottom of a page.

4. Amend the spacing before and after the **Subtitle** style to **6pt** and **12pt** respectively.

5. Apply a **1½pt** red box border to the title and paragraph **Overview**.

6. Apply a **1½pt** orange box border to the title and paragraph **Celebration Food**.

7. Highlight **Day 15** and its associated text in the **Rituals** section with bright green.

8. Shade the very last paragraph of text with 20% grey.

9. Save the document as **Chinese New Year3** and close it.

10. Open the document **Topperville Hall**.

11. Apply a **¼pt** black box border to the paragraph of text about Elizabeth in the paragraph about **The House**.

12. Apply the same border to the text of the first paragraph about **The Gardens**.

13. On page 2, apply a **1pt** blue shadow border to the final 2 paragraphs, about the **Tea Room**.

14. Print the document.

15. Save the document as **Borders**.

16. Close it.

Advanced Printing

These exercises include topics taken from the following list: printing odd and even pages, printing selected text and printing specific pages.

Exercise 5

1. Open the document **Computer Info**.

2. Go to the last page of the document and print this page only.

3. Print pages **1** to **3** and **8** only.

4. Print the even pages so that two pages are printed on every sheet.

5. Print the section about networks.

6. Print the section about computer viruses.

7. Print only the information about extranets on page **10**.

8. Close the document without saving.

Exercise 6

1. Open the document **Swimming** and print only the odd pages.

2. Print the table on page **4** only.

3. Print only the text which gives information about the currently available activities (starts page **5**).

4. Print the chart on page **7** and then close the document without saving.

5. Open the document **Chinese New Year**.

6. Print the paragraph about **The Years** and the associated table.

7. Print the paragraph about **Celebration Food**.

8. Close the document without saving.

Document Layout

These exercises include topics taken from the following list: adding and deleting section breaks, applying shading to parts of a document, creating multiple columns in a document, modifying column layout and width & spacing.

Exercise 7

1. Open the document **Topperville Hall**.

2. Insert continuous section breaks in the following locations:

   Before the first paragraph (not the heading) of **The Gardens** text.

   Before the text of the **Pets' Corner** paragraph.

   Before the **Gift Shop** heading.

3. Apply 2 columns to the **Gardens** section.

4. Change the spacing between the columns to **0.7cm**.

5. Force a new page before the **Pets' Corner** heading.

6. Apply 3 columns to the **Pets' Corner** text.

7. Change the column width to **3.75cm** and the column spacing to **0.5cm**.

8. Increase the spacing before the **Gift Shop** heading to **12pt**.

9. Apply a **1pt** dark green shadow border to the paragraph and heading about **The House**.

10. Apply light grey shading to the **Gardens** and **Pets' Corner** sections.

11. Apply a **1pt** dark green shadow border to the whole document.

12. Save the document as **Topperville Hall3** and close it.

Exercise 8

1. Open the document **Computer Info**.

2. Insert continuous section breaks in the following locations:

   a) Before the heading **About the Personal Computer**.

   b) Before the heading **About IT**.

   c) Before the heading **About Input and Output Devices**.

   d) Before the heading **About Storing Information**.

e) Before the second paragraph in **About Storing Information**.

f) Before the heading **About Files**.

g) Before the heading **About Networks**.

h) Before the heading **About the Internet…**.

i) Before the heading **About Viruses**.

3. Apply 2 columns to the text (not the heading) referring to input and output devices.

4. In the paragraph **About Storing Information**, apply 2 columns to the section beneath the table.

5. Make sure a line separates these columns.

6. Change the spacing between columns to **0.5cm**.

7. The **Intranets** heading is now at the bottom of page 9 and is separated from the rest of the paragraph. Apply a setting to keep the heading and paragraph together.

8. Click **OK**.

9. Shade all of the text referring to viruses.

10. Apply a border of your choice to the bulleted text about anti-virus measures.

11. Save the document as **Computer Formatting** and close it.

Tables

These exercises include topics taken from the following list: merging and splitting cells, converting text to a table, sorting data, performing calculations.

Exercise 9

1. Start a new document and create a table to match the one below, to record attendance of a group of trainee soldiers on a variety of army assault courses.

Week Commencing:				
Soldier ID	Course 1	Course 2	Course 3	Course 4
Number of successful completions:				

2. Save the document as **Squaddies** and close it.

3. Start another new document and create the following table. Include the shading.

Regional warehouse location:			
Part No.	**No. in Stock**	**Item value**	**Total**
Total Stock Value:			

4. Enter 8 records to complete the table.

5. Use a calculation to sum the total stock value in the bottom right cell.

6. Save the document as **Stock** and print a copy of the table.

7. Close the document.

Exercise 10

1. Start a new document.

2. Enter the text shown below, separating each item by pressing <**Tab**>.

Surname	First Name	Department	Annual Salary
Johnson	Robert	Catering	11,500
Singh	Indira	Personnel	18,750
Abdul	Jenny	IT Support	25,179
Franks	Peter	Personnel	16,275
Butler	Jane	Training	19,100
Harrison	Susan	Catering	11,500
Roper	Billy	IT Support	24,500

3. Convert the text to a table, separating by tabs.

4. Format the top row of the table as bold and centre align all of the text.

5. Sort the data in ascending alphabetical order by surname.

6. Add an extra row at the bottom of the table.

7. Merge cells 1 to 3 in this row and enter the text **Sum of Annual Salary**.

8. Right align the text in this cell and make it bold.

9. In the fourth cell on the bottom row, perform an automatic addition calculation to add up salaries paid for the year.

10. Save the document as **Salaries**.

11. Close the document.

Text Boxes

These exercises include topics taken from the following list: inserting and deleting text boxes, editing text boxes, moving and resizing text boxes, applying borders to text boxes, linking text boxes.

Exercise 11

1. Open the document **Republic**.

2. Centre the main heading and change the font to **Arial 14pt** bold.

3. Change all of the remaining text to **Arial**, with the paragraph headings as **12pt**, bold and the body text **10pt**, regular.

4. Place the first paragraph of text inside a text box and reduce the width of the text box to about **8cm**.

5. Ensure all of the text is displayed.

6. Move the text box into the second section, **Power Struggle** and make the text wrap to the right of the text box.

7. Create a second text box around the paragraphs relating to **Emperor**.

8. Widen the text box until it spans the margins, but decrease its depth so that only the first paragraph of text is visible.

9. Draw a third text box at the bottom right of the page.

10. Link it to the second, **Emperor**, box.

11. Move this last box beneath the second one, at the right of the page and make it about half the width of the page.

12. Extend this box downward until all of the text it contains can be seen, but ensure that there is not too much white space displayed.

13. Apply blue **1½pt** borders to the text boxes.

14. Move the boxes on the page, so that all text can be clearly seen.

15. Spell check the document.

16. Save the document as **Boxes** and close it.

Exercise 12

1. Start a new, blank document.

2. Press <**Ctrl Enter**> to create a second page.

3. On each page, draw a text box to fill about half of the page.

4. Place the cursor inside the text box on page **1** and select **Insert | File**.

5. Insert the file **Topperville Hall** from the data location.

6. Create a link between the text boxes and ensure the remainder of the text is displayed in the second frame on page **2**.

7. Resize the boxes so that the paragraph heading **The Garden** begins at the top of the text box on page **2**.

8. On page **1**, move the text box to the bottom of the page and insert the picture **stately_home.gif** from the data files.

9. Increase the size of the graphic until it is approximately treble its original size and move it above the text box, ensuring it is positioned centrally.

10. At the very top of the page, create graphical text to say **History of Topperville Hall**. Move this to the top centre of the page.

11. Delete the title from the text box and increase the size of the italicised text to **14pt**.

12. Ensure the text box on page **2** still starts with the heading **The Gardens**.

13. Insert the picture **flower.gif** on to page **2**.

14. Reduce it to about half its original size and position it at the bottom right of the page.

15. Print the document.

16. Save the document as **Hall** and close it.

Graphics & Drawing

These exercises include topics taken from the following list: modifying graphic borders, using graphic editing software, creating a simple drawing, aligning, grouping and layering objects, creating a watermark.

Exercise 13

1. Open the document **Graphics**.

2. Edit the graphics as specified below (right click on the object and select **Picture Object | Open**):

Skier	change her sweater to pink and her trousers to blue (each area of the clothing will have to be edited separately).
Leaves	change the green leaf to red and the largest leaf to yellow.
Snowman	change his hat to 2 shades of purple, e.g. purple and lavender, using the lighter shade on those areas that are currently lighter.
Dog	change the collar to green, the barrel to gold and the tongue to pale pink.

3. Give each graphic a border and fill colour, or fill effect, of your choice.

4. If any graphic overlaps another one, move them apart.

5. Save the document as **Graphics2** and close it.

Exercise 14

1. Start a new document.

2. Create the drawing shown below to act as the first page. The text is created using **WordArt**.

3. When the drawing is complete, group all of its components.

4. Insert the text file **Sunny.doc**, ensuring it starts at the top of a new page.

5. Create a watermark from the data file **sunny**

6. Save the document as **Sunny2** and close it.

Referencing

These exercises include topics taken from the following list: creating, modifying & deleting footnotes & endnotes, changing footnote & endnote options, creating, formatting & updating a table of contents, adding & deleting bookmarks, creating & deleting cross-references, adding captions, changing caption options, creating & editing index entries.

Exercise 15

1. Open the document **Computer Info**.

2. Amend the **Section** style to be outline level 1 (**Format | Style**, **Modify**, **Format | Paragraph**).

3. Change the headings that are bold (not the italic section headings) to **Heading 2** style.

4. Amend the **Heading 2** style paragraph spacing to **6pt** before and after.

5. Create a new page at the beginning of the document and insert a table of contents, **Simple** format, showing 2 levels: **Section** at level 1 and **Heading 2** at level 2.

6. Above the table of contents, type **Contents** and format the text as **Times New Roman 18pt** bold, centred.

7. At the end of the document, force a new page and type **Index**, same format as above.

8. Create the index by marking all occurrences of:

   PC, **Laptop**, **PDA**, **network**, **mainframe**, **device**, **IT**, **CPU**, **storage**, **drive**, **file**, **directory**, **folder**, **performance**, **Internet**, **intranet**, **extranet**, **e-mail**, **virus**.

9. The index should also have the **Simple** format applied.

10. Use a function key to refresh the table of contents and remove index marks from it.

11. Your manager has asked you to give a short talk about networks, but you feel you need to brush up. Bookmark the following text:

About Networks heading	page 9
ISDN	page 10
PSTN	page 10
ADSL	page 10

12. Test the bookmarks.

13. Save the document as **Computer Info2** and close it.

Exercise 16

1. Open the document **Swimming**.

2. On page **3**, insert the following footnote after the word **timetable** in the Introduction: **see the table overleaf for more details**.

3. Convert all the footnotes to endnotes.

4. The second endnote is no longer appropriate. Delete it.

5. After the text **timetable** on page **3**, type **(see table** and insert a cross-reference to the table (**Table 1**), which shows the pool activities. Complete the reference by closing the brackets.

6. Insert captions below each graphic on pages 1 to 5, with the following text (you will need to make the graphic on page **1** slightly smaller):

Page **1**	**Family friendly**
Page **3**	**Serious swimmers welcome**
Page **3**	**View from café**
Page **5**	**Swimming lessons**.

*Note: The captions beneath the floating graphics on page **1** and **5** will be in text boxes. This is OK.*

7. Save the document as **Swimming2** and close it.

Templates

These exercises include topics taken from the following list: modifying a template, creating a new template.

Exercise 17

1. Open the template **Company Fax.dot** from the data files.

2. Replace the globe watermark with the picture **grapes.gif** from the data files.

3. Resize the picture to about half its original size.

4. Move the picture until it is at the left of the **Notes** area of the fax.

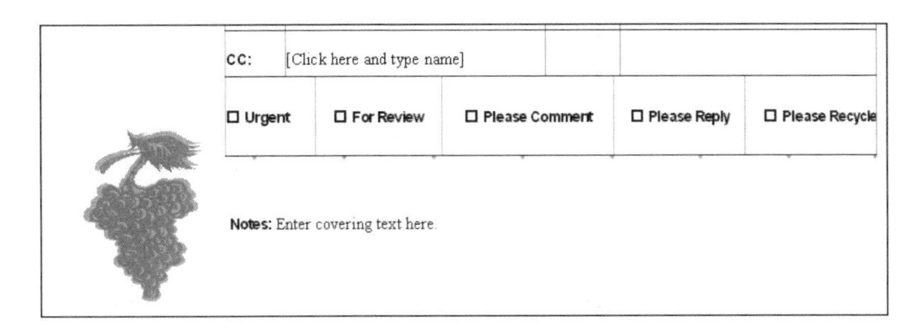

CC: [Click here and type name]

☐ Urgent ☐ For Review ☐ Please Comment ☐ Please Reply ☐ Please Recycle

Notes: Enter covering text here.

5. The company has moved to larger premises, **Unit 9**. Make the change on the fax.

6. Change the font of the address text to italic, **12pt**.

7. Change the banner **facsimilie transmittal** to **FAX**.

8. Save the fax as a template, to the default location, as **Company Fax2.dot**.

9. Close the document.

Exercise 18

1. Open the document **Marine Zoology**. You are a biology teacher and have decided that this document can be used as the basis for a variety of lecture notes.

2. Create the following styles:

Title1	Arial, bold, 16pt, centred, space after 12pt.
Title2	Arial, bold, 12pt, left, space before 6pt, after 6pt.
Textstyle	Arial 10pt, justified, 1.5 line spacing, space after 6pt

3. Apply the **Title1** style to the title **Sharks**.

4. Apply the **Title2** style to the subheadings.

5. Apply the **Textstyle** to the body text.

6. Remove any extra paragraph marks.

7. Change the main title text to **Name of Species**.

8. Delete the heading **Teeth** and the associated text.

9. Leave all other headings as they are, but replace their associated text with **Relevant text here**.

10. Delete the graphic in the header and add a centred header of **Biology Lectures Year 10**. Format the text as **Arial 10pt bold**.

11. Insert centred page numbers in the footer.

12. Apply pencils border art, **12pt** to the page.

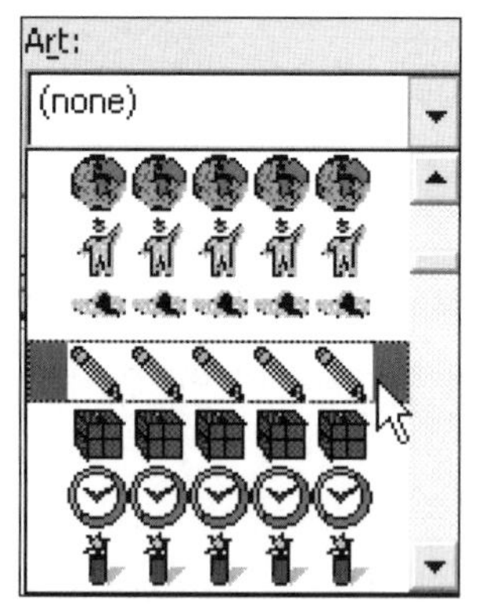

13. Save the file as a template, to the default location, as **Lecture.dot**.

Collaborative Editing

These exercises include topics taken from the following list: adding and removing comments, edit comments, tracking changes to a document, accepting or rejecting changes.

Exercise 19

1. Open the document **Chinese New Year**.

2. After **...a different date each year...** in the first sentence, insert a comment which reads **January or February**.

3. Add the following comments to the table on page 1, next to the name of the animal:

Rat	generous, imaginative, charming, quick tempered
Ox	natural leader, methodical, dexterous
Tiger	adventurous, brave, charming, shows initiative, impulsive
Rabbit	pleasant, co-operative, affectionate, sentimental
Dragon	popular, vivacious, fun loving
Snake	thoughtful, romantic, wise, charming
Horse	very hardworking, independent, intelligent, friendly
Sheep	charming, artistic, elegant, a worrier
Monkey	popular, intelligent, successful
Rooster	hardworking, forthright, makes firm decisions
Dog	faithful, honest, a worrier
Boar	tolerant, honest, a good friend

4. Edit the comment about the tiger - replace **impulsive** with **a risk taker**.

5. Delete the comment in the first sentence.

6. Save the document as **New Year Comments**.

Exercise 20

1. Open the document **Wonders**.

2. Turn on tracking.

3. Increase the size of the main title to **20pt**.

4. In paragraph 3 on page 1, replace **mastabas** with **tombs known as mastabas**.

5. On the final paragraph on page 2, insert a new sentence after sentence 1: **It is also thought to have been used as target practice during World War II.**

6. Print the document showing the changes.

7. Move to the start of the document.

8. Work through the editing; accept the first change to the font size.

9. Accept the change to the sentence about mastabas.

10. Reject the change about target practice.

11. Save the document as **Wonders2** and close it.

Document Security

These exercises include topics taken from the following list: password protecting a document, changing passwords, removing passwords.

Exercise 21

1. Open the document **Sunny**.
2. Change security settings so that a password (**openme**) is required to open the document.
3. Change settings to prevent unauthorised changes to the document, using the password **changeme**.

4. Save the document as **Secured** and then close it.
5. Reopen the document **Secured**, entering the correct passwords.
6. Which of the passwords will enable you to make editing changes?
7. Embolden the final sentence and save the changes to the document using the same name, i.e. **Secured**.
8. Close the document.

Exercise 22

1. Open the document **Nursery**. This document has the password **security** applied.
2. Change the password required to open the document to **safety**.
3. Save the document as **Nursery2** and close it.

4. Check the new password has taken effect by opening the document **Nursery2** again.

5. Remove all password protection from the document and save it using the same name.

6. Check that password protection has been successfully removed, then close the document.

Master Documents

These exercises include topics taken from the following list: creating a master document, creating a subdocument, adding or removing a subdocument.

Exercise 23

1. Create a new, master document with the title **Egyptian Odyssey Holidays**.

2. Beneath the title, enter the following (normal level) text: **Choose an Egyptian Odyssey holiday and you will be amazed at the excursions you can take. Read this document for some examples.**

3. Insert the following files as subdocuments, in the order shown, to compose elements of the master document:

    Pyramid_Sphinx
    Luxor
    Valleys
    Balloon Trip
    Nile Cruise

4. Remove the section break on page **1** and in **Normal** view ensure there are no blank pages. In **Outline** view, ensure the subdocuments are expanded.
5. Save the completed document as **Trips**.
6. Close any open documents.

Exercise 24

1. Open the document **Excursions**. This is a completed master document.
2. The balloon trip is no longer offered by the holiday company. Remove it from the master document, but leave the master document open.
3. In place of the balloon trip, the company is now offering scuba diving. Start a new document and insert the text file **Scuba.txt**.
4. Format the title as **Forte 18pt** dark red centred, the subtitle as **Arial Black 12pt** dark red centred and the body text as **Arial 11pt**, black, justified.
5. Insert the graphic **scubadiving** and position it between the second and third paragraphs.
6. Centre the graphic and ensure there is a **12pt** space above and below it.
7. Save this new document as **Diving** and close it.
8. Insert **Diving** as a subdocument, after the **Valleys** subdocument.
9. Save the amended master document as **Trips2**.
10. Print out the section on diving only.
11. Close any open documents.

Field Codes and Forms

These exercises include topics taken from the following list: inserting, deleting, editing and updating field codes, locking or unlocking a field, creating and editing a form, changing form field options, protecting and deleting form fields

Exercise 25

1. Open the document **Survey**.
2. Change the red bullets to black numbers and apply a tab at **12cm** to each numbered line. Make sure the numbers are sequential across all lists.
3. For questions **1**, **3**, **4**, **5**, **6**, **7** and **9**, add a field at the tab position, allowing the options **Yes** or **No**.
4. For question **2**, add a field with the available options **Yes**, **No, too warm**, **No, too cold**.
5. For question 8, the options should be **Yes**, **No**, **Don't know**.
6. For the bulleted list, insert fields that allow text entry, at a **6cm** tab position.
7. Limit the number of characters allowed for a name to **30**, ensuring the name will always appear in title case.
8. Add a checkbox at the end of the form, after the word **box**.
9. Ensure the form layout can't be changed inadvertently.
10. Save the form as **Survey2** and close it.

Exercise 26

1. Open the document **Fieldcodes**.
2. In the header, insert a right aligned field code which will show the author's name.
3. Which key press would lock this field to prevent updates?
4. Amend the field in the footer to show only the file name.
5. Insert page breaks before the **Great Pyramid** and **Red Sea Diving** headings.
6. Update the page numbers in the table of contents.
7. Delete the field in the header.
8. Replace it with a code that will show the current date each time the document is opened.
9. Ensure all field codes are displayed.
10. Save the document as **Fieldcodes2** and close it.

Mail Merge

These exercises include topics taken from the following list: editing a mail merge data source, sorting a data source, using different data sources

Exercise 27

1. Open the document **Party**. This is a mail merge document. If a prompt about **SQL** appears click **Yes**.

2. View the **Recipients List** from the data source (**Members**), which is linked to the document. You may need to search in the data files for the data source.

3. Sort the data by surname in descending alphabetical order.

4. **Maddy Mustard** has cancelled her membership. Amend the records accordingly.

5. **The Barnacles** have moved to **7 Chapel Drive**, **Riverside**, **Noplace**. Make the necessary changes.

6. Print the merged records.

7. Complete the merge to a new document.

8. Save the merged file as **New Members**.

9. Close all open documents.

Exercise 28

1. Open the document **Exhibition**. If a prompt about **SQL** appears click **Yes**.

2. This document is linked to the data source **Teachers**. You may need to search in the data files for the data source if prompted. View the list of potential recipients.

3. Sort the data source alphabetically by school.

4. Which school is at the bottom of the list?

5. You have been supplied with the wrong list of teachers; it is a list of language teachers, not IT coordinators. Use the **IT_Teachers** data source instead.

6. Continue the merge process and preview the letters. How many are there?

7. Save the merged file as **IT Exhibition**.

8. Close any other open documents without saving.

Working with Spreadsheets

These exercises include topics taken from the following list: modifying an embedded chart, creating a chart from a worksheet, modifying a chart

Exercise 29

1. In a new, blank document, use **Insert | Object** to insert the spreadsheet **Maintenance**, ensuring the data for the whole year is visible (this may mean changing the page setup).

2. You have just received a memo detailing extra work done in July, amounting to **250**. Amend the worksheet accordingly.

3. Create a 3-D clustered column chart from the data, to appear as an object on the worksheet.

4. The chart title is **Maintenance Contracts** and the value axis title is **Amount**.

5. Position the chart centrally beneath the data and ensure all of the chart data is displayed.

6. The chart data series should display the actual values, but no legend should be visible.

7. Ensure the value axis scale starts at **400**.

8. Update the data in the spreadsheet for October to **1175** and ensure the chart also reflects this change.

9. Save the file as **Costs**.

10. Close the document.

Exercise 30

1. Open the document **Woodland Lodges**.

2. Insert the spreadsheet **Lodges** beneath the sentence **Prices for the current year...** and ensure all of the data is displayed.

3. Apply a **6pt** space above the extract.

4. Create a bar chart from the data in the spreadsheet extract. The chart title is **Tariff**. The scale for the figures is to start at **100**.

5. Ensure all the data for March to October is displayed, but do not display a legend.

6. Change the colour of the data series to pale green, the plot area to olive green and the chart area to pale yellow.

7. Change the font of the chart title to **Tahoma** and the category axis to italic.

8. Apply a **1pt** olive green box border to the extract.

9. Save the document as **Woodland Lodges2**.

10. Close the document.

Macros

These exercises include topics taken from the following list: recording a macro, running a macro, copying a macro, assigning a button to a macro.

Exercise 31

1. Open the document **Balloon Macro**.
2. Create a macro named **Watermark** within this document only that will insert the picture file **map_of_egypt** as a printed watermark.
3. Save the amended document as **Balloon Macro2**.
4. Copy the macro to the document **Pyramid_Sphinx2**.
5. Assign the macro to a button with a pencil picture (4th row).
6. Save the amended document as **Pyramid_Sphinx3**.
7. Run the macro.
8. Remove the button from the toolbar and delete the macro from the document.
9. Save the amendments.
10. Close all open documents.

Exercise 32

1. Open the document **Space Shuttle Intro**.
2. Create a macro, stored in this document only, called **Orientation**. The macro should change the page layout to **Landscape**.

3. Assign the macro to a button with the image of a book (6th row).

4. Ensure the document is in **Portrait** and test the macro using the button.

5. Create a second macro named **Signoff**, within the current document, that will add your name and job title (you are a rocket scientist) on two lines at the end of the document, e.g.

   Bob Farina

   Rocket Scientist

6. Place the cursor at the end of the text and test the macro.

7. Copy the macros to the document **Marine Biology**.

8. Run the macro **Orientation**.

9. Close **Marine Biology** without saving.

10. Delete the **Signoff** macro from **Space Shuttle Intro**.

11. Save the document as **Space Shuttle Intro2**.

12. Close the document.

General Exercises

The following revision exercises can involve processes from any part of the ECDL advanced syllabus.

Exercise 33

1. Open the document **Space Shuttle Intro**. Apply small caps and the font colour dark red to the second line, **Reproduced by permission...**.

2. Attach a comment to **destroyed in an explosion during ascent in January 1986** in paragraph 2. The comment is to read **7 crew members were lost**.

3. Without moving it, format the space shuttle image at the bottom of page 1 so that the text wraps tightly around the left side of the image only.

4. Delete the extra paragraph mark left where the image was originally, ensuring the text remains justified.

5. Remove the widow and orphan setting on the last paragraph on page 1, which ensures the last line will never appear on its own at the top of a page.

6. Create a new style named **Body**, based on the **Normal** style. This style is **Arial 11pt**, with **12pt** space before and after the paragraph. Apply the **Body** style to all text with the exception of the first two lines (headings).

7. On page 2, apply a **1pt** shadow border around the paragraph starting **Since 1992...**. This paragraph should also have 5% shading in grey.

8. Insert a caption that reads **Image 1** beneath the orbiter flight configuration image.

9. On page 2, create a heading above the paragraph **NASA is prepared...**, which reads **Conclusion**. Format this heading as **Arial 12pt**, bold and change the font colour to dark teal.

10. Add a bookmark called **summingup** to the **Conclusion** heading.

11. The names of the space shuttle orbiters are to be made bold and italic and have their colour changed to dark red. Create a macro named **orbiters**, in this document only, to perform these actions on any selected text.

12. Assign the macro to a button on the **Standard** toolbar, with a pencil icon. Use the button to format the orbiters' names on page 1, paragraph 1 and 2, and on page 2, paragraph 3 (**Conclusion**).

13. Insert a right aligned field in the header to show the filename. In the centre of the footer, insert a field to show the current date and time. Lock the field in the header.

14. Add a footnote to the text **orbit** in the first sentence. The footnote should read **The course around the earth followed by the shuttle**. Adjust the position of the lower image if necessary.

15. Apply a password to open the document (**space**) and a different password (**nasa**) to make any changes.

16. Save the file as **Space Shuttle2** and close it.

17. Open the document **Space Shuttle2** and type your name at the end of the text to ensure the passwords to open and modify have been applied.

18. Save the changes to the document and close it.

Exercise 34

1. Open the document **Locations**. Apply a shadow effect to the title.

2. Format the image so that the text wraps tightly to its left edge, but do not move it.

3. Edit the comment attached to the first bullet point to read **You should at least know the basics**.

4. Turn on tracking. Edit the footnote on page 1 by changing **edges** to **boundaries**.

5. Amend the **Paragraph Heading** style so that the associated text is always kept with the heading. Ensure this style is always followed by the **Text** style.

6. Amend the **Bullets** style so that the bullet colour is red.

7. In the **Costs** paragraph on page 2, change **when buying a property** to **when buying a property abroad**.

8. Insert a new paragraph heading at the end of the text with the text **Buyers on the increase**. Enter the associated text **The chart below shows the steady rise in the number of owners of property abroad**.

9. Insert the spreadsheet extract from the file **Graph**, centre it and create an embedded line chart from the data (this data is invented). The chart title is **Foreign Property Owners** and the value axis text is **Thousands**. Ensure all of the data is displayed.

10. Change the chart area colour to pale blue and ensure no legend is displayed.

11. Change the minimum value axis scale to **10**.

12. Save the file as **Locations2** and close it (the tracked changes are not accepted/rejected to ensure evidence of them remains).

13. Open the document **Property**. If a prompt about **SQL** appears, click **Yes**. This main document is attached to the data source **Buyers**. You may need to search in the data file location for it.

14. Sort the data source in alphabetical order by **Last Name** and then complete the merge, saving to a new file called **New Buyers**. Close the merged file and the **Property** file (without saving).

15. Copy the following styles from the **Locations** document to **Feedback** (if you know how to copy styles using the **Organizer**, then use this method; alternatively open **Locations**, make a note of the formatting of each of the styles, then set them up in **Feedback**): **Paragraph Heading**, **Bullets** and **Text**.

16. Apply the **Paragraph Heading** style to the first line, **Home Seekers Abroad**. Apply the **Bullets** style to all of the questions and the **Text** style to the remaining text.

17. In **Feedback**, add a further item - **Property magazine** - to the drop down list associated with **Where did you hear about the company?**

18. Add a tab at **10.5cm** to the bullets only. Insert a check box after the last word in the document, **box**.

19. Ensure the form data is protected and save as **Feedback2**. Close any open files.

Exercise 35

1. Open the document **Marine Zoology** and edit the graphic in the header as follows: change the man's hair to brown and his suit to dark green.

2. Replace the title **Sharks** with **WordArt** text, using the same text and the fourth style on the fourth row. Move the text to the top left of the page, ensuring it is at the same height as the graphic on the right.

3. Animate the text **Do not panic...** in the **Conclusion** with a shimmer effect.

4. Apply the **Heading 1** style to the **Introduction** heading and **Heading 2** style to the remaining headings. Create a new style, **Main Body**, based on the **Normal** style, **Arial 11pt** justified, **6pt** after, body text level. Apply this style to the remaining text.

5. Promote the **Heading 2** headings to level 1 throughout the document.

6. Insert a table of contents before the **Introduction** heading, using the **Formal** format, showing 2 levels. Insert a page break after the table of contents.

7. Demote the headings that were promoted in step 5 back to level 2. Update the table of contents to show these changes.

8. Mark all occurrences of the names of shark species (**blue shark**, **great white shark**, **swellshark**, **Port Jackson shark**, **mako**, **Basking**, **whale**, **megamouth** and **grey nurse**) throughout the document as index entries. Do not mark the references to body form, i.e. **typical**, **mackerel**, **cat shark**.

9. Force a new page at the end of the document and type the heading **Index** formatted as **Heading 1**. Create an index on this new page, beneath the heading, using the **Formal** format. Update the table of contents so that the index is shown.

10. Place the **Introduction** text (not the heading) within a text box. Apply a dark blue **1pt** border to the text box and fill it with a blue tissue paper effect. The text box should be positioned beneath the **Introduction** title at the top of the page.

11. Ensure the **Conclusion** and associated text start at the top of page 4. Put this text, including the heading, into a text box formatted the same as the one on page 2. The text box should be positioned at the top of page 4.

12. Format the text between the boxes in 2 columns. Ensure each column is **6cm** wide and that there is a line between the columns.

13. Create a watermark for the document using the file **sea.gif**. Ensure the image is not washed out and that its scale is **400%** (type in the value).

14. Ensure all entries in the table of contents and index are current.

15. Save the file as **Marine Zoology3** and close it.

Exercise 36

1. Open the document **Shrubbies**. This is a new staff newsletter for a garden centre.

2. Change settings so that whenever the letters **SGC** are typed, they are automatically replaced by **Shrubbies Garden Centre**.

3. At the end of the document, in the **Safety and Maintenance** section, add a final point on a new line: **SGC will not accept responsibility for accidents arising from disregard of these instructions**.

4. Create a new style, **Bulletpoints**, based on the **Text** style, but with a dark green bullet that looks like a flower or leaf.

5. Apply the new style to the text in the **Safety and Maintenance** section.

6. Place the **Plant of the Month** article on the first page inside a text box. Apply a **1½ pt** dark green border to the text box.

7. Reduce the size of the picture of the orange tree so that the table at the bottom of the page is not pushed on to page 2.

8. In the sales table on page 1, merge the cells on the top row and centre the title. Make it bold and italic. Embolden the titles on row 2 and the **Grand Total** row.

9. Insert a formula in the empty **Grand Total** cell, which will return the value of all sales.

10. On page 2, beneath the spreadsheet extract, create an embedded 3-D column chart. The value axis should have the title **Number Sold**.

11. Change the chart area to pale green and the walls to mid green. All text on the chart must be **Comic Sans**, **9pt**, italic.

12. Add the following comment to the chart: **OT: ornamental trees, CT: citrus trees, E: evergreens, FS: flowering shrubs, F: flowers, FT: fruit trees, IP: indoor plants**.

13. Add this comment to point 3 in the **Safety and Maintenance** section: **Do not place cacti or venus fly traps where small children may reach them**. Ensure all comments in this document are hidden.

14. Apply a setting so that a caption is automatically inserted below each new graphic, using the label **Image**.

15. On page 3, insert a suitable clip art image in the herb section, after the **Coriander** paragraph and before the **Oregano** paragraph.

16. Ensure the image is in line with the text and centred. The image should be approximately **3cm** x **2½cm**. If you cannot find a clip, use **herb.gif** from the data files.

17. Ensure the **Safety and Maintenance** section starts at the top of page 4. Insert a second suitable clip art image in this section, between the first and second bullet points, again ensuring the image is centred and in line with the text. If you cannot find a clip, use the image **tools.gif** from the data files.

18. The image should be approximately **4cm**x **2½cm**. Do not worry if the caption has moved away from the graphic.

19. Add a field to the right of the header, to insert the current date in English format.

20. Apply a security setting, so that the newsletter may only be edited if a password is supplied. The password is **potter**.

21. Save the document as **Shrubbies2**. Close the document and then reopen it to check the security setting is working.

22. Print only the **How to...** section, including the herb information, then save and close the document.

Exercise 37

1. Start a new, blank document, which is to act as a template for a customer questionnaire. The company offers several services and wants all of their questionnaires to have a corporate look.

2. Create a company logo like the one shown opposite, using drawing shapes and layering techniques. When complete, ensure none of the components can be moved individually. Ensure the logo is no more than **2cm** high and move it to the centre of the header.

3. Set all page margins to **2.5cm**. Create the following styles:

Heading	Based on normal style, followed by **Maintext**, Arial 14pt bold, left aligned, 6pt before, 12pt after

Maintext Based on normal style, Arial, 11pt, justified, 6pt after

Bullets Based on **Maintext**, bulleted with the ➢ symbol.

4. At the top of the page, select the **Heading** style and type **Heading goes here**. Beneath this type **This is the style for the main body text** (if you have set the styles up correctly this should already be formatted). On the next line type **Bulleted text uses the Bullet style**. Apply the appropriate style.

5. Modify the **Heading** style to be centred. Save the document as a template in the **Templates** folder with the name **Corporate1** and close it.

6. Start a new document based on the **Corporate1** template and create the questionnaire shown below. The first three questions use **Yes/No** drop down lists, the fourth uses a text field and the fifth uses a **Yes/No/Don't know** drop down list. The remaining fields are text fields.

Good Idea!

Customer Satisfaction Questionnaire - Sparkle Cleaning Services

You have recently used Sparkle Cleaning Services for the first time.

As a valued new customer, we would appreciate you taking the time to answer the following questions:

- Did your cleaner arrive on time? Yes
- Did they spend the agreed amount of time at your premises? Yes
- Were you satisfied with the standard of cleaning? Yes
- If not, why not?
- Will you be using the service again? Yes

For our records, please supply the following information:

Name:

Company:

Telephone:

e-mail:

Thank you for taking the time to complete the questionnaire. Please return it in the enclosed prepaid envelope.

General Exercises

7. Add a footnote to the second question about the amount of time spent: **The agreed time can be found on your contract.**

8. Protect the form so that deletions cannot be made. Save the file as **Sparkle**.

9. Open the document **Response**. This is a completed questionnaire returned by a customer.

10. Add a comment to the third response: **Interview the cleaner about these comments**.

11. Save the document as **Response2** and close it.

12. Delete the **Corporate1** template.

Exercise 38

1. Open the document **Locations**. Amend the styles as follows: **Text** - **Verdana 11pt**, **Bullets** - **Verdana 11pt** italic, **Paragraph Heading** - **Verdana 12pt** bold.

2. Ensure the **Professional Help** heading is kept with the associated text.

3. Apply columns to the **Costs** and **Making an offer** paragraphs and associated text.

4. Ensure the text **If you are not regularly living** starts at the top of column 2, using a column break.

5. Shade the text in columns with a 5% shade of grey.

6. Reduce the spacing between columns to **1cm**.

7. On page **2**, use drawing tools to create a sun, measuring approximately **3cm** x **3cm**.

8. Fill the object with a 2 colour gradient effect, using light yellow and gold, shaded from the centre. Choose the paler variant option.

9. Make the sun 70% transparent and arrange it so that it appears behind the text and is right aligned.

10. Save the document as **Locations Edit** and close it.

11. Open the document **Feedback**. You have received instructions from head office to remove references to currently owning property abroad.

12. Delete the questions **Do you currently own property abroad?** and **If so, in which country?** and their associated form fields.

13. Protect the form, save it as **Feedback Edit** and close it.

14. A mailshot has previously been sent to new members of the property club **Home Seekers Abroad**. However, you have just been informed that the Smalltown letters have been blown away in a gale. Open the file **Property** (attached to the data source **Buyers**).

15. Filter the recipient list and create a mail merge which will only be sent to Smalltown residents.

16. Save the merge file as **Smalltown** and close all open files. Do <u>not</u> save the changes to **Property**.

17. Create a new master document. This is to act as a starting point for an information booklet, with sections for various locations. Using the **Heading 1** style, type **Information for Buyers**.

18. On the next line using the **Normal** style, type **Please refer to the relevant section for the country you are interested in**.

19. Beneath this, using the **Heading 2** style, type **France**. On the following line, in **Normal** style, type **Content about France here**. Select these two lines and create a subdocument from them.

20. Create further subdocuments, following the above pattern, for **Spain**, **USA**, **Australia** and **New Zealand**.

21. Save the completed master document as **Buyers Info** and close it.

This section contains answers to all specific questions posed in the preceding exercises, together with the name of the file or files containing the worked solution for each exercise.

Exercise 1

A sample solution for this exercise is saved as **Chinese New Year2 Solution** in the **Word Processing Solutions** folder.

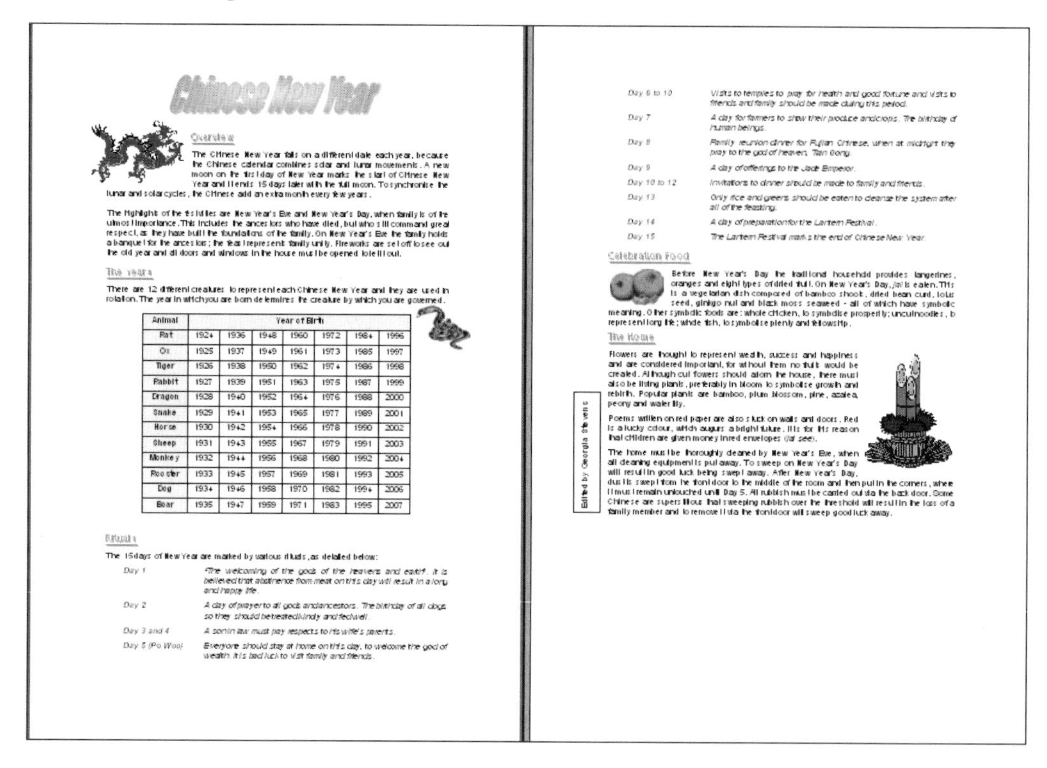

Chinese New Year

Overview

The Chinese New Year falls on a different date each year, because the Chinese calendar combines solar and lunar movements. A new moon on the first day of New Year marks the start of Chinese New Year and it ends 15 days later with the full moon. To synchronise the lunar and solar cycles, the Chinese add an extra month every few years.

The highlights of the festivities are New Year's Eve and New Year's Day, when family is of the utmost importance. This includes the ancestors who have died, but who still command great respect, as they have built the foundations of the family. On New Year's Eve the family holds a banquet for the ancestors; the feast represents family unity. Fireworks are set off to see out the old year and all doors and windows in the house must be opened to let it out.

The years

There are 12 different creatures to represent each Chinese New Year and they are used in rotation. The year in which you are born determines the creature by which you are governed.

Animal	Year of Birth						
Rat	1924	1936	1948	1960	1972	1984	1996
Ox	1925	1937	1949	1961	1973	1985	1997
Tiger	1926	1938	1950	1962	1974	1986	1998
Rabbit	1927	1939	1951	1963	1975	1987	1999
Dragon	1928	1940	1952	1964	1976	1988	2000
Snake	1929	1941	1953	1965	1977	1989	2001
Horse	1930	1942	1954	1966	1978	1990	2002
Sheep	1931	1943	1955	1967	1979	1991	2003
Monkey	1932	1944	1956	1968	1980	1992	2004
Rooster	1933	1945	1957	1969	1981	1993	2005
Dog	1934	1946	1958	1970	1982	1994	2006
Boar	1935	1947	1959	1971	1983	1995	2007

Rituals

The 15 days of New Year are marked by various rituals, as detailed below:

Day 1	*"The welcoming of the gods of the heavens and earth". It is believed that abstinence from meat on this day will result in a long and happy life.*
Day 2	*A day of prayer to all gods and ancestors. The birthday of all dogs, so they should be treated kindly and fed well.*
Day 3 and 4	*A son in law must pay respects to his wife's parents.*
Day 5 (Po Woo)	*Everyone should stay at home on this day, to welcome the god of wealth. It is bad luck to visit family and friends.*
Day 6 to 10	*Visits to temples to pray for health and good fortune and visits to friends and family should be made during this period.*
Day 7	*A day for farmers to show their produce and crops. The birthday of human beings.*
Day 8	*Family reunion dinner for Fujian Chinese, when at midnight they pray to the god of heaven, Tian Gong.*
Day 9	*A day of offerings to the Jade Emperor.*
Day 10 to 12	*Invitations to dinner should be made to family and friends.*
Day 13	*Only rice and greens should be eaten to cleanse the system after all of the feasting.*
Day 14	*A day of preparation for the Lantern Festival.*
Day 15	*The Lantern Festival marks the end of Chinese New Year.*

Celebration Food

Before New Year's Day the traditional household provides tangerines, oranges and eight types of dried fruit. On New Year's Day, *jai* is eaten. This is a vegetarian dish composed of bamboo shoots, dried bean curd, lotus seed, ginkgo nut and black moss seaweed - all of which have symbolic meaning. Other symbolic foods are: whole chicken, to symbolise prosperity; uncut noodles, to represent long life; whole fish, to symbolise plenty and fellowship.

The Home

Flowers are thought to represent wealth, success and happiness and are considered important, for without them no fruit would be created. Although cut flowers should adorn the house, there must also be living plants, preferably in bloom to symbolise growth and rebirth. Popular plants are bamboo, plum blossom, pine, azalea, peony and water lily.

Poems written on red paper are also stuck on walls and doors. Red is a lucky colour, which augurs a bright future. It is for this reason that children are given money in red envelopes (*lai see*).

The home must be thoroughly cleaned by New Year's Eve, when all cleaning equipment is put away. To sweep on New Year's Day will result in good luck being swept away. After New Year's Day, dust is swept from the front door to the middle of the room and then put in the corners, where it must remain untouched until Day 5. All rubbish must be carried out via the back door. Some Chinese are superstitious that sweeping rubbish over the threshold will result in the loss of a family member and to remove it via the front door will sweep good luck away.

Edited by Georgia Stevens

Exercise 2

Sample solutions for this exercise are saved as **Topperville Hall2 Solution** (not shown below) and **Marine Zoology2 Solution** in the **Word Processing Solutions** folder.

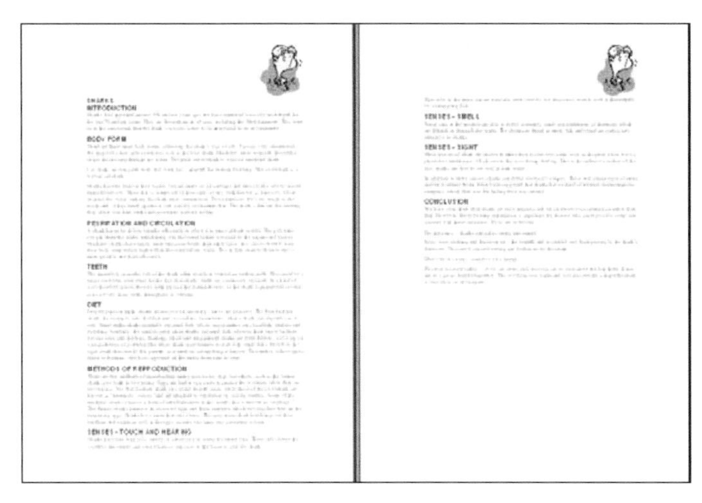

Exercise 3

A sample solution for this exercise is saved as **Republic Outline Solution** in the **Word Processing Solutions** folder. You are required to obtain a printout showing the levels in the document, because when it is reopened (as in the solution file) they will not be on view.

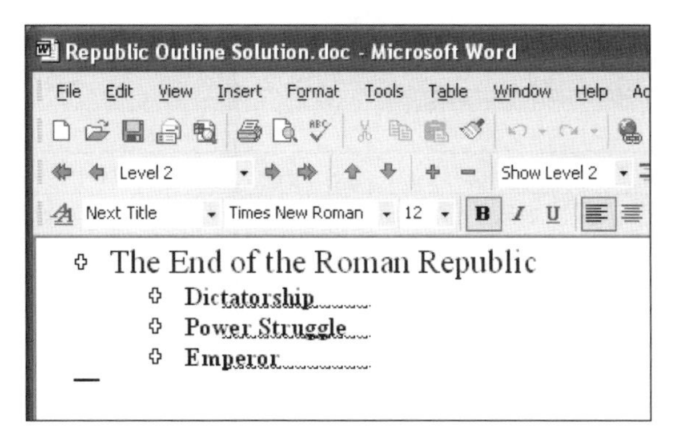

Exercise 4

Sample solutions for this exercise are saved as **Chinese New Year3 Solution** and **Borders Solution** in the **Word Processing Solutions** folder.

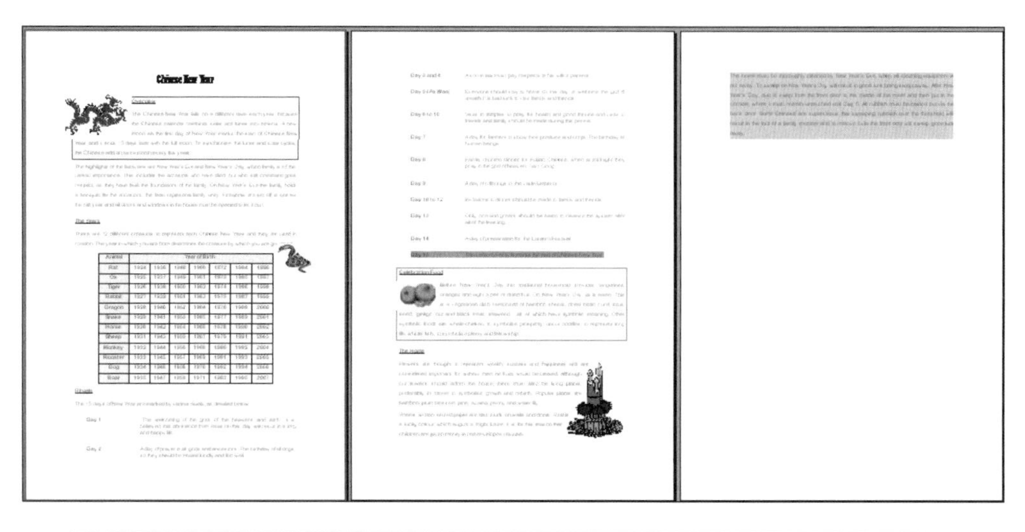

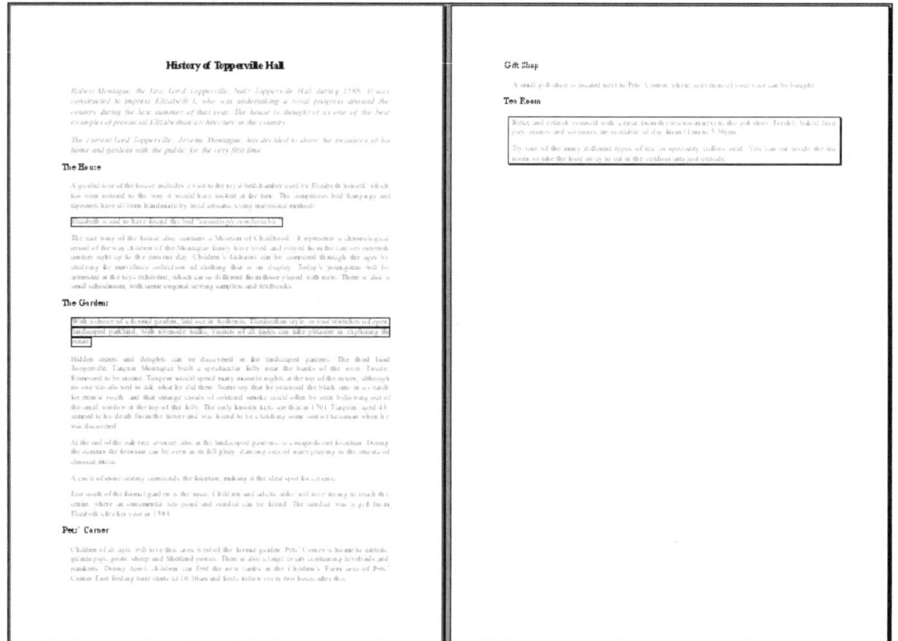

Exercise 7

A sample solution for this exercise is saved as **Topperville Hall3 Solution** in the **Word Processing Solutions** folder.

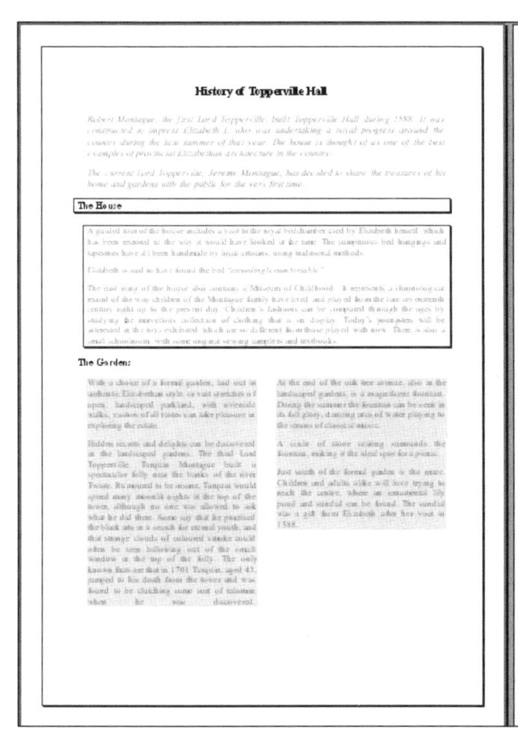
History of Topperville Hall

The House

The Gardens

Pets' Corner

Gift Shop

Tea Room

Exercise 8

A sample solution for this exercise is saved as **Computer Formatting Solution** in the **Word Processing Solutions** folder.

Exercise 10

A sample solution for this exercise is saved as **Salaries Solution** in the **Word Processing Solutions** folder.

Exercise 11

A sample solution for this exercise is saved as **Boxes Solution** in the **Word Processing Solutions** folder.

The End of the Roman Republic

Dictatorship

In 45BC, after more than 450 years as a republic, Rome was turned into a dictatorship when the soldier and politician Julius Caesar seized power. Staunch republicans in the senate accused Caesar of having delusions of grandeur and aspirations to become an absolute and divine monarch. Although he did in fact enlarge the senate, they thought his ambition would deprive them of power and democracy. As a result, Caesar made many powerful enemies. These men and others with grievances formed a conspiracy and plotted to overthrow Caesar. This group, led by Cassius and Brutus, murdered Caesar in the senate on the Ides of March (15th) 44BC.

Power Struggle

The assassination of Caesar ignited 14 years of civil war. From 44 to 31BC there ensued a power struggle between Julius Caesar's heir Octavian and Marc Antony (although Caesar had a son with Cleopatra - Caesarion - he had named Octavian as his successor in his will).

Finally, after Antony and Cleopatra were defeated at the Battle of Actium in 31BC and committed suicide, Octavian was left as the sole ruler of the Roman Empire, including Egypt.

Emperor

Perhaps learning from Julius Caesar's mistakes, Octavian did not make himself dictator of Rome, but instead in 27BC founded a monarchy headed by emperors. Octavian changed his name to Augustus, keeping the prefix Caesar.

Augustus began a programme of social reform and building works, also becoming a patron to poets such as Horace and Virgil. However, although towards the end of his life Augustus claimed to have restored the republic, he ensured his position as emperor would pass to a successor (his stepson Tiberius). From then until the fall of the Roman Empire, Rome was ruled by an emperor and not by the senate and its people, meaning that the republic did indeed end with Julius Caesar.

Exercise 12

A sample solution for this exercise is saved as **Hall Solution** in the **Word Processing Solutions** folder.

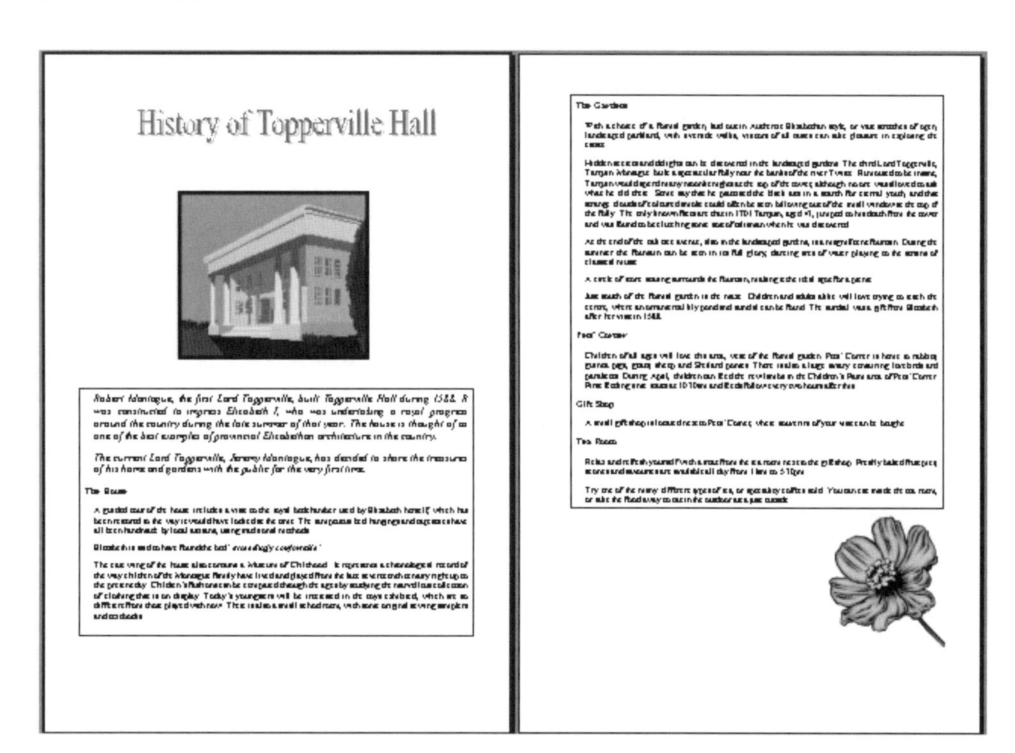

Exercise 13

A sample solution for this exercise is saved as **Graphics2 Solution** in the **Word Processing Solutions** folder

Exercise 14

A sample solution for this exercise is saved as **Sunny2 Solution** in the **Word Processing Solutions** folder.

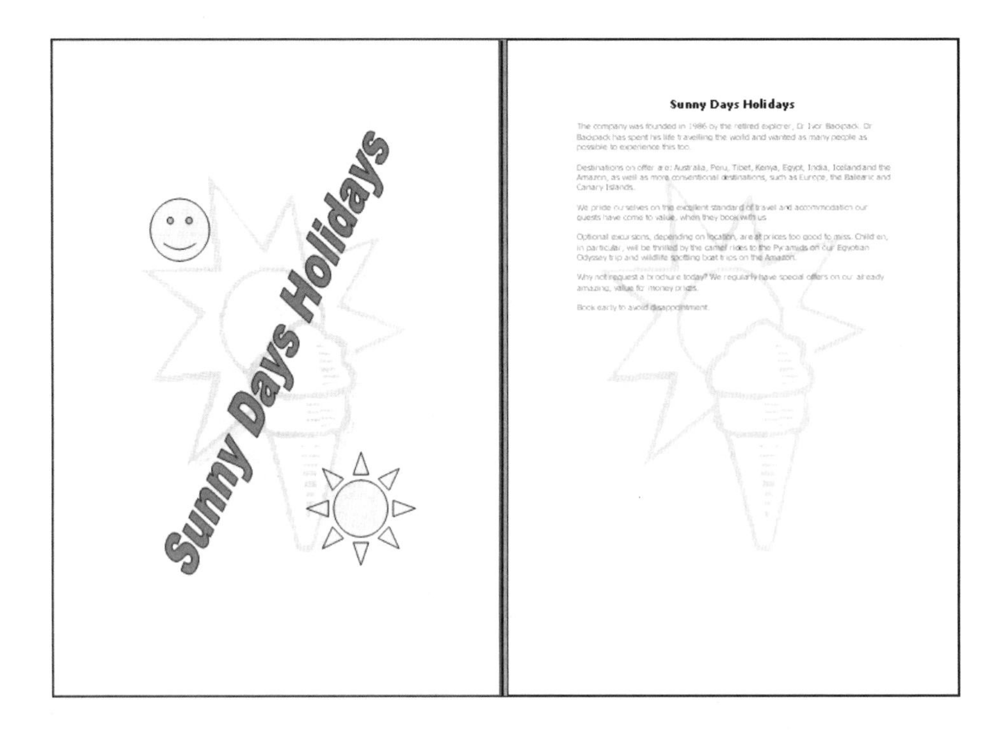

Exercise 15

A sample solution for this exercise is saved as **Computer Info2 Solution** in the **Word Processing Solutions** folder.

Exercise 16

A sample solution for this exercise is saved as **Swimming2 Solution** in the **Word Processing Solutions** folder.

Exercise 17

A sample solution for this exercise is saved as **Company Fax2 Solution.dot** in the **Word Processing Solutions** folder.

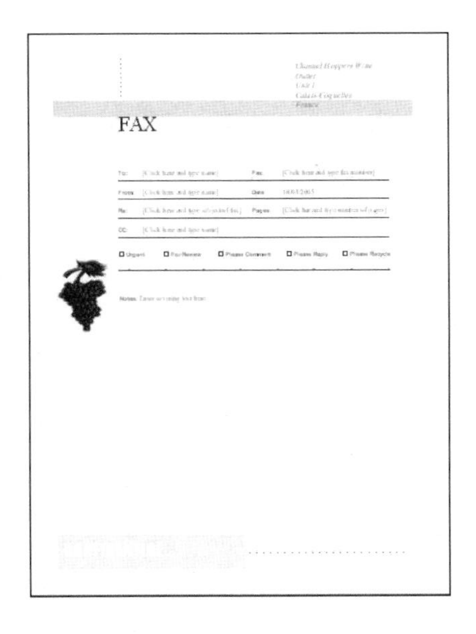

FAX

Exercise 18

A sample solution for this exercise is saved as **Lecture Solution.dot** in the **Word Processing Solutions** folder.

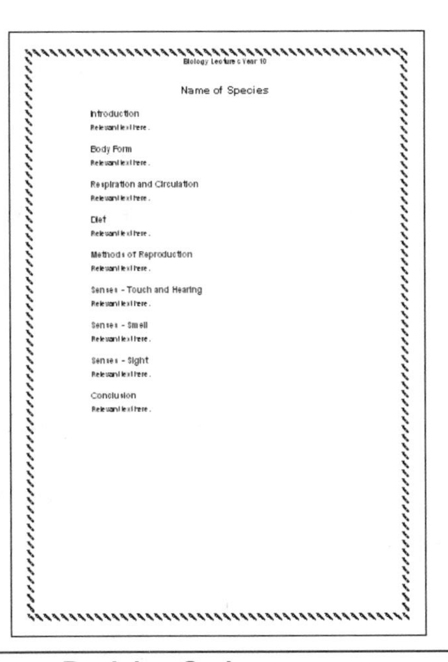

Biology Lectures Year 10

Name of Species

Introduction

Relevant text here.

Body Form

Relevant text here.

Respiration and Circulation

Relevant text here.

Diet

Relevant text here.

Methods of Reproduction

Relevant text here.

Senses - Touch and Hearing

Relevant text here.

Senses - Smell

Relevant text here.

Senses - Sight

Relevant text here.

Conclusion

Relevant text here.

Exercise 19

A sample solution for this exercise is saved as **New Year Comments Solution** in the **Word Processing Solutions** folder.

The Years

There are 12 different creatures to represent each Chinese New Year and they are used in rotation. The year in which you are born determines the creature by which you are governed.

Animal	Year of Birth						
Rat	1924	1936	1948	1960	1972	1984	1996
Ox	1925	1937	1949	1961	1973	1985	1997
Tiger	1926	1938	1950	1962	1974	1986	1998
Rabbit	1927	1939	1951	1963	1975	1987	1999
Dragon	1928	1940	1952	1964	1976	1988	2000
Snake	1929	1941	1953	1965	1977	1989	2001
Horse	1930	1942	1954	1966	1978	1990	2002
Sheep	1931	1943	1955	1967	1979	1991	2003
Monkey	1932	1944	1956	1968	1980	1992	2004
Rooster	1933	1945	1957	1969	1981	1993	2005
Dog	1934	1946	1958	1970	1982	1994	2006
Boar	1935	1947	1959	1971	1983	1995	2007

Comment: Generous, imaginative, charming, quick tempered

Comment: Natural leader, methodical, dexterous

Comment: Adventurous, brave, charming, shows initiative, a risk taker

Comment: Pleasant, co-operative, affectionate, sentimental

Comment: Popular, vivacious, fun loving

Comment: Thoughtful, romantic, wise, charming

Comment: Very hardworking, independent, intelligent, friendly

Comment: Charming, artistic, elegant, a worrier

Comment: Popular, intelligent, successful

Comment: Hardworking, forthright, makes firm decisions

Comment: Faithful, honest, a worrier

Comment: Tolerant, honest, a good friend

Rituals

The 15 days of New Year are marked by various rituals, as detailed below:

Day 1 "The welcoming of the gods of the heavens and earth". It is believed that abstinence from meat on this day will result in a long and happy life.

Day 2 A day of prayer to all gods and ancestors. The birthday of all dogs, so they should be treated kindly and fed well.

Exercise 20

A sample solution for this exercise is saved as **Wonders2 Solution** in the **Word Processing Solutions** folder.

Exercise 21

Step 7 The password required to modify the document is **changeme**.

A sample solution for this exercise is saved as **Secured Solution** in the **Word Processing Solutions** folder.

Exercise 23

A sample solution for this exercise is saved as **Trips Solution** in the **Word Processing Solutions** folder.

Exercise 24

Examples of the output from this exercise are saved as **Diving Solution** and **Trips2 Solution** in the **Word Processing Solutions** folder.

Exercise 25

Step 3 - <**Ctrl F11**>.

A sample solution for this exercise is saved as **Survey2 Solution** in the **Word Processing Solutions** folder.

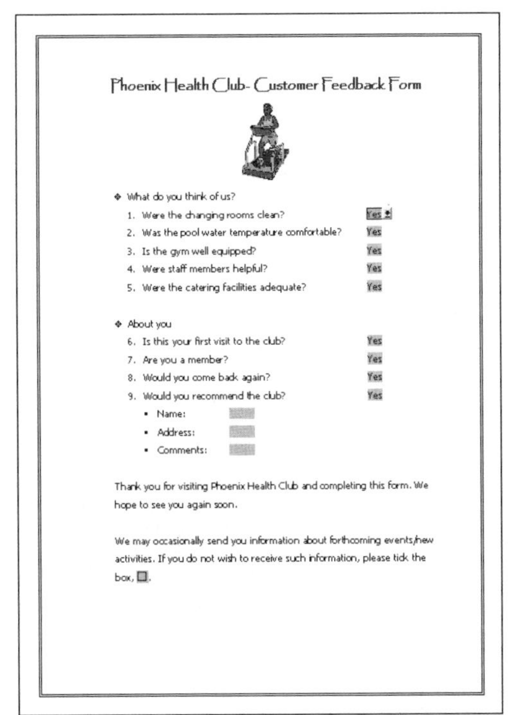

Phoenix Health Club- Customer Feedback Form

- What do you think of us?
  1. Were the changing rooms clean? Yes
  2. Was the pool water temperature comfortable? Yes
  3. Is the gym well equipped? Yes
  4. Were staff members helpful? Yes
  5. Were the catering facilities adequate? Yes

- About you
  6. Is this your first visit to the club? Yes
  7. Are you a member? Yes
  8. Would you come back again? Yes
  9. Would you recommend the club? Yes
     - Name:
     - Address:
     - Comments:

Thank you for visiting Phoenix Health Club and completing this form. We hope to see you again soon.

We may occasionally send you information about forthcoming events/new activities. If you do not wish to receive such information, please tick the box, ☐.

Exercise 26

A sample solution for this exercise is saved as **Fieldcodes2 Solution** in the **Word Processing Solutions** folder.

Exercise 27

A sample solution for this exercise is saved as **New Members Solution** in the **Word Processing Solutions** folder.

Exercise 28

Step 3 St Peter's Primary.

Step 5 There are 9 letters.

A sample solution for this exercise is saved as **IT Exhibition Solution** in the **Word Processing Solutions** folder.

Exercise 29

A sample solution for this exercise is saved as **Costs Solution** in the **Word Processing Solutions** folder.

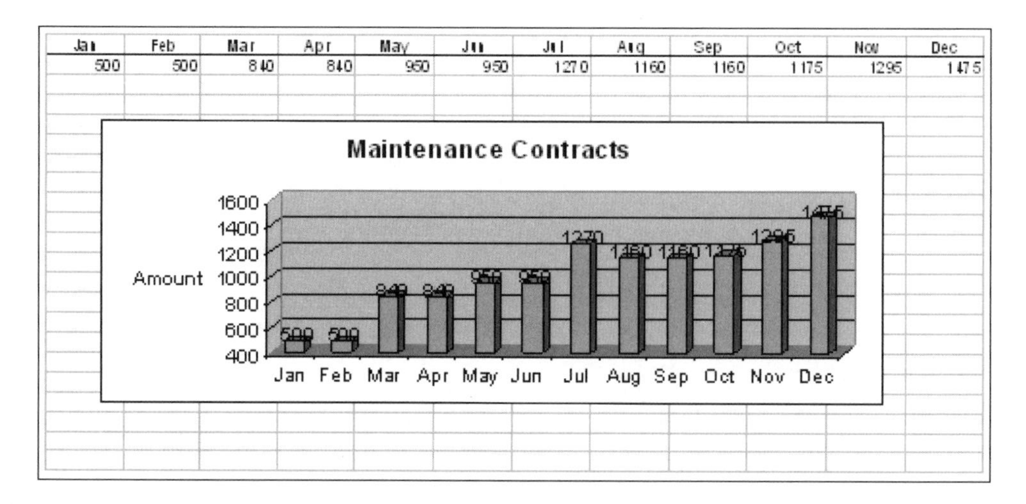

Jan	Feb	Mar	Apr	May	Jun	Jul	Aug	Sep	Oct	Nov	Dec
500	500	840	840	950	950	1270	1160	1160	1175	1295	1475

Exercise 30

A sample solution for this exercise is saved as **Woodland Lodges2 Solution** in the **Word Processing Solutions** folder.

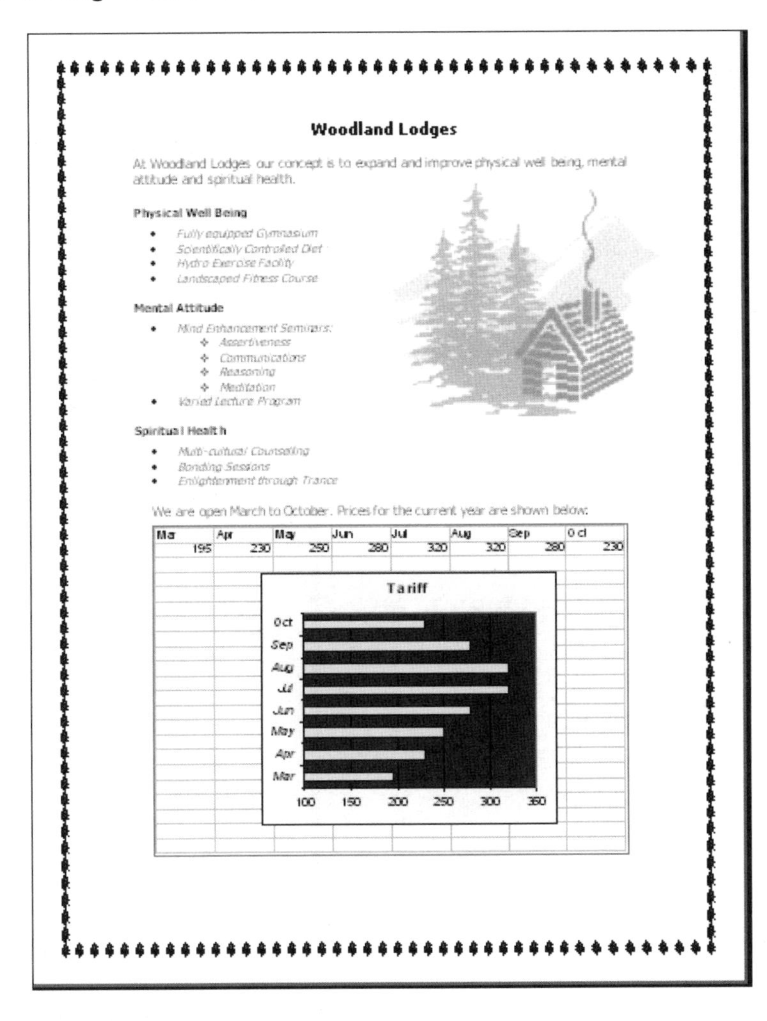

Woodland Lodges

At Woodland Lodges our concept is to expand and improve physical well being, mental attitude and spiritual health.

Physical Well Being

- *Fully equipped Gymnasium*
- *Scientifically Controlled Diet*
- *Hydro Exercise Facility*
- *Landscaped Fitness Course*

Mental Attitude

- *Mind Enhancement Seminars:*
    - *Assertiveness*
    - *Communications*
    - *Reasoning*
    - *Meditation*
- *Varied Lecture Program*

Spiritual Health

- *Multi-cultural Counselling*
- *Bonding Sessions*
- *Enlightenment through Trance*

We are open March to October. Prices for the current year are shown below:

Mar	Apr	May	Jun	Jul	Aug	Sep	Oct
195	230	250	280	320	320	280	230

Exercise 31

Examples of the output from this exercise are saved as **Balloon Macro2 Solution** and **Pyramid_Sphinx3 Solution** in the **Word Processing Solutions** folder.

Exercise 32

A sample solution for this exercise is saved as **Space Shuttle Intro2 Solution** in the **Word Processing Solutions** folder.

Exercise 33

A sample solution for this exercise is saved as **Space Shuttle2 Solution** in the **Word Processing Solutions** folder.

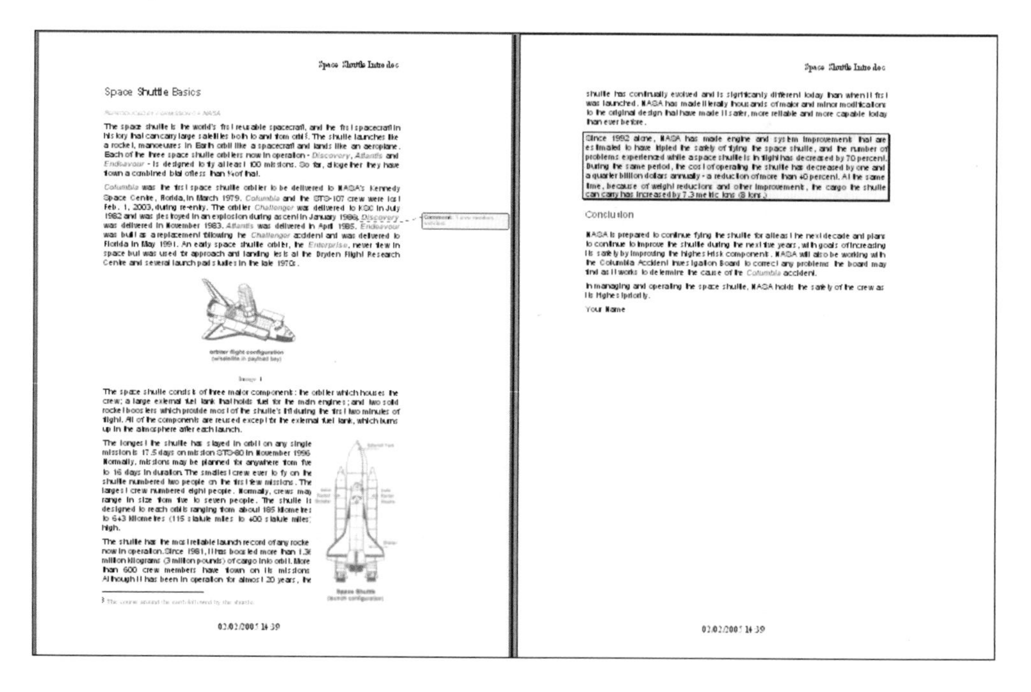

Space Shuttle Intro.doc

Space Shuttle Basics

The space shuttle is the world's first reusable spacecraft, and the first spacecraft in history that can carry large satellites both to and from orbit³. The shuttle launches like a rocket, manoeuvres in Earth orbit like a spacecraft and lands like an aeroplane. Each of the three space shuttle orbiters now in operation - *Discovery*, *Atlantis* and *Endeavour* - is designed to fly at least 100 missions. So far, altogether they have flown a combined total of less than ¼ of that.

Columbia was the first space shuttle orbiter to be delivered to NASA's Kennedy Space Centre, Florida, in March 1979. *Columbia* and the STS-107 crew were lost Feb. 1, 2003, during re-entry. The orbiter *Challenger* was delivered to KSC in July 1982 and was destroyed in an explosion during ascent in January 1986. *Discovery* was delivered in November 1983. *Atlantis* was delivered in April 1985. *Endeavour* was built as a replacement following the *Challenger* accident and was delivered to Florida in May 1991. An early space shuttle orbiter, the *Enterprise*, never flew in space but was used for approach and landing tests at the Dryden Flight Research Centre and several launch pad studies in the late 1970s.

The space shuttle consists of three major components: the orbiter which houses the crew; a large external fuel tank that holds fuel for the main engines; and two solid rocket boosters which provide most of the shuttle's lift during the first two minutes of flight. All of the components are reused except for the external fuel tank, which burns up in the atmosphere after each launch.

The longest the shuttle has stayed in orbit on any single mission is 17.5 days on mission STS-80 in November 1996. Normally, missions may be planned for anywhere from five to 16 days in duration. The smallest crew ever to fly on the shuttle numbered two people on the first few missions. The largest crew numbered eight people. Normally, crews may range in size from five to seven people. The shuttle is designed to reach orbits ranging from about 185 kilometres to 643 kilometres (115 statute miles to 400 statute miles) high.

The shuttle has the most reliable launch record of any rocket now in operation. Since 1981, it has boosted more than 1.36 million kilograms (3 million pounds) of cargo into orbit. More than 600 crew members have flown on its missions. Although it has been in operation for almost 20 years, the

02/02/2005 14:39

Space Shuttle Intro.doc

shuttle has continually evolved and is significantly different today than when it first was launched. NASA has made literally thousands of major and minor modifications to the original design that have made it safer, more reliable and more capable today than ever before.

Since 1992 alone, NASA has made engine and system improvements that are estimated to have tripled the safety of flying the space shuttle, and the number of problems experienced while a space shuttle is in flight has decreased by 70 percent. During the same period, the cost of operating the shuttle has decreased by one and a quarter billion dollars annually - a reduction of more than 40 percent. At the same time, because of weight reductions and other improvements, the cargo the shuttle can carry has increased by 7.3 metric tons (8 tons.)

Conclusion

NASA is prepared to continue flying the shuttle for at least the next decade and plans to continue to improve the shuttle during the next five years, with goals of increasing its safety by improving the highest risk components. NASA will also be working with the Columbia Accident Investigation Board to correct any problems the board may find as it works to determine the cause of the *Columbia* accident.

In managing and operating the space shuttle, NASA holds the safety of the crew as its highest priority.

Your Name

02/02/2005 14:39

Exercise 34

Sample solutions for this exercise are saved as **Locations2 Solution**, **New Buyers Solution** (not shown) and **Feedback2 Solution** in the **Word Processing Solutions** folder.

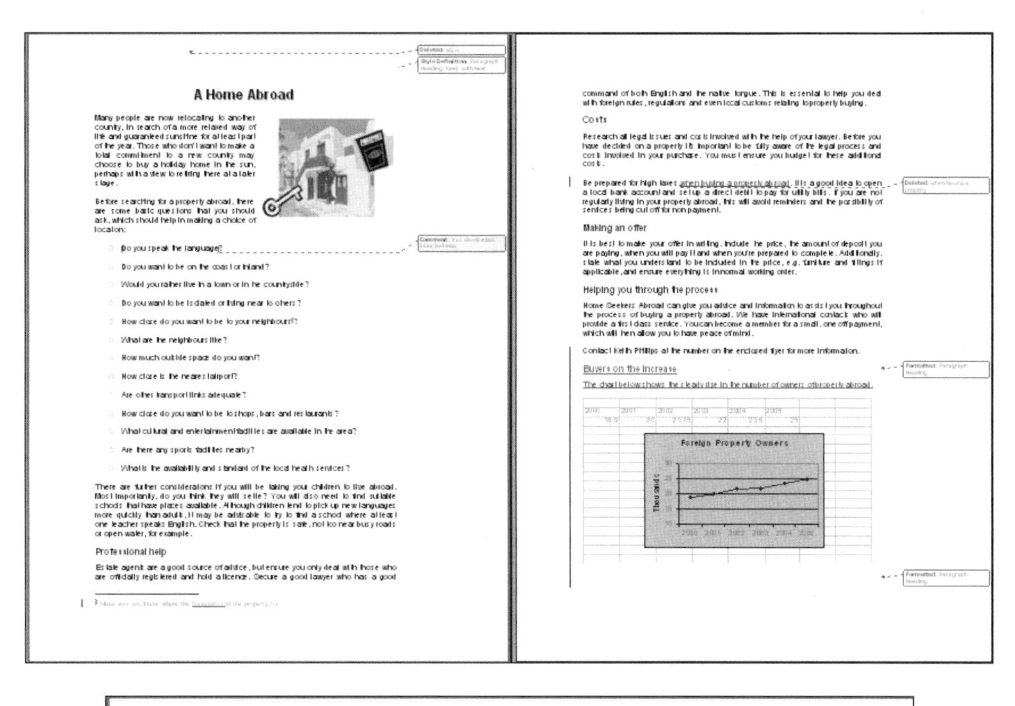

A Home Abroad

Many people are now relocating to another country, in search of a more relaxed way of life and guaranteed sunshine for at least part of the year. Those who don't want to make a total commitment to a new country may choose to buy a holiday home in the sun, perhaps with a view to retiring there at a later stage.

Before searching for a property abroad, there are some basic questions that you should ask, which should help in making a choice of location:

- Do you speak the language?
- Do you want to be on the coast or inland?
- Would you rather live in a town or in the countryside?
- Do you want to be isolated or living near to others?
- How close do you want to be to your neighbours?
- What are the neighbours like?
- How much outside space do you want?
- How close is the nearest airport?
- Are other transport links adequate?
- How close do you want to be to shops, bars and restaurants?
- What cultural and entertainment facilities are available in the area?
- Are there any sports facilities nearby?
- What is the availability and standard of the local health services?

There are further considerations if you will be taking your children to live abroad. Most importantly, do you think they will settle? You will also need to find suitable schools that have places available. Although children tend to pick up new languages more quickly than adults, it may be advisable to try to find a school where at least one teacher speaks English. Check that the property is safe, not too near busy roads or open water, for example.

Professional help

Estate agents are a good source of advice, but ensure you only deal with those who are officially registered and hold a licence. Secure a good lawyer who has a good command of both English and the native tongue. This is essential to help you deal with foreign rules, regulations and even local customs relating to property buying.

Costs

Research all legal issues and costs involved with the help of your lawyer. Before you have decided on a property it's important to be fully aware of the legal process and costs involved in your purchase. You must ensure you budget for these additional costs.

Be prepared for high taxes when buying a property abroad. It is a good idea to open a local bank account and set up a direct debit to pay for utility bills. If you are not regularly living in your property abroad, this will avoid reminders and the possibility of services being cut off for non payment.

Making an offer

It is best to make your offer in writing. Include the price, the amount of deposit you are paying, when you will pay it and when you're prepared to complete. Additionally, state what you understand to be included in the price, e.g. furniture and fittings if applicable, and ensure everything is in normal working order.

Helping you through the process

Home Seekers Abroad can give you advice and information to assist you throughout the process of buying a property abroad. We have international contacts who will provide a first class service. You can become a member for a small, one off payment, which will then allow you to have peace of mind.

Contact Keith Phillips at the number on the enclosed flyer for more information.

Buyers on the Increase

The chart below shows the steady rise in the number of owners of property abroad.

2000	2001	2002	2003	2004	2005
18.5	20	21.75	22	23.5	25

Home Seekers Abroad

To help us with market research, please take a few moments to answer the following questions:

- Where did you hear about the company? Internet search
- Do you currently own property abroad? Yes
- If so, in which country?
- What type of property are you looking to buy? House or villa
- Do you want a property with a pool? Yes
- Does the property have to be detached? Yes
- Are you looking near the coast or inland? Inland
- Do you want a rural or urban property? Rural
- Are you prepared to renovate? Yes
- Please supply your e-mail address

Thank you for taking the time to complete his questionnaire.

Please indicate if you would like us to e-mail you our monthly newsletter by checking the box. ☐

Exercise 35

A sample solution for this exercise is saved as **Marine Zoology3 Solution** in the **Word Processing Solutions** folder.

Exercise 36

A sample solution for this exercise is saved as **Shrubbies2 Solution** in the **Word Processing Solutions** folder.

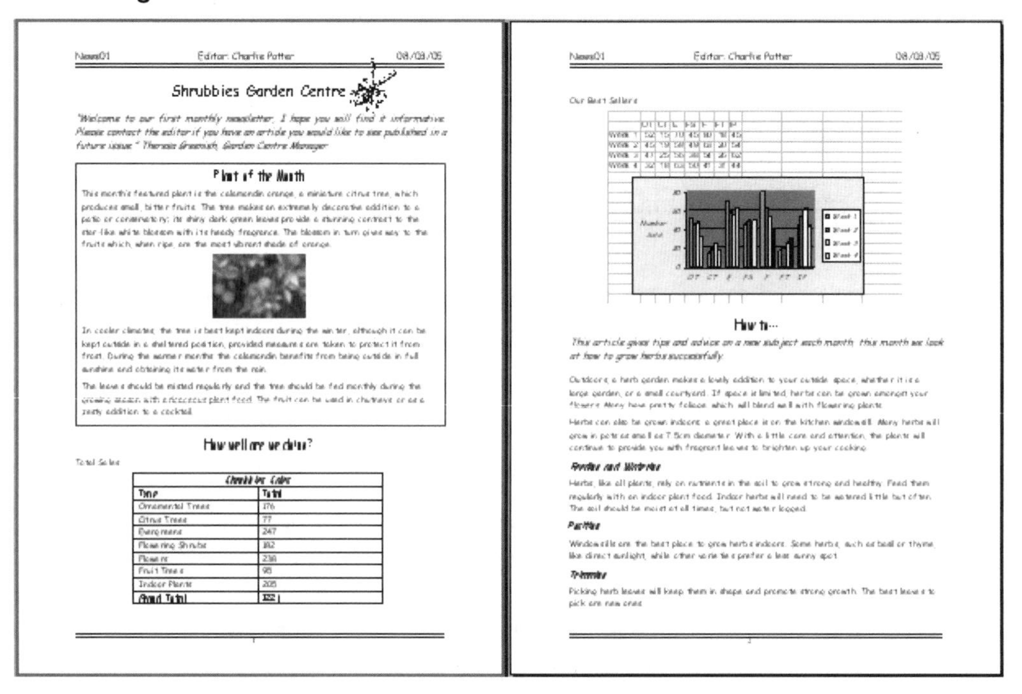

News01 Editor: Charlie Potter 08/08/05

Shrubbies Garden Centre

"Welcome to our first monthly newsletter. I hope you will find it informative. Please contact the editor if you have an article you would like to see published in a future issue." Theresa Greenwich, Garden Centre Manager

Plant of the Month

This month's featured plant is the calamondin orange, a miniature citrus tree, which produces small, bitter fruits. The tree makes an extremely decorative addition to a patio or conservatory; its shiny dark green leaves provide a stunning contrast to the star-like white blossom with its heady fragrance. The blossom in turn gives way to the fruits which, when ripe, are the most vibrant shade of orange.

In cooler climates, the tree is best kept indoors during the winter, although it can be kept outside in a sheltered position, provided measures are taken to protect it from frost. During the warmer months the calamondin benefits from being outside in full sunshine and obtaining its water from the rain.

The leaves should be misted regularly and the tree should be fed monthly during the growing season with ericaceous plant feed. The fruit can be used in chutneys or as a zesty addition to a cocktail.

How well are we doing?

Total Sales

Shrubbies Sales	
Type	Total
Ornamental Trees	176
Citrus Trees	77
Evergreens	247
Flowering Shrubs	182
Flowers	238
Fruit Trees	98
Indoor Plants	205
Grand Total	[illegible]

News01 Editor: Charlie Potter 08/08/05

Our Best Sellers

How to...

This article gives tips and advice on a new subject each month; this month we look at how to grow herbs successfully.

Outdoors, a herb garden makes a lovely addition to your outside space, whether it is a large garden, or a small courtyard. If space is limited, herbs can be grown amongst your flowers. Many have pretty foliage which will blend well with flowering plants.

Herbs can also be grown indoors; a great place is on the kitchen windowsill. Many herbs will grow in pots as small as 7.5cm diameter. With a little care and attention, the plants will continue to provide you with fragrant leaves to brighten up your cooking.

Feeding and Watering

Herbs, like all plants, rely on nutrients in the soil to grow strong and healthy. Feed them regularly with an indoor plant feed. Indoor herbs will need to be watered little but often. The soil should be moist at all times, but not waterlogged.

Position

Windowsills are the best place to grow herbs indoors. Some herbs, such as basil or thyme, like direct sunlight, while other varieties prefer a less sunny spot.

Trimming

Picking herb leaves will keep them in shape and promote strong growth. The best leaves to pick are new ones.

Exercise 37

Sample solutions for this exercise are saved as **Sparkle Solution** and **Response2 Solution** in the **Word Processing Solutions** folder.

Customer Satisfaction Questionnaire - Sparkle Cleaning Services

You have recently used Sparkle Cleaning Services for the first time.

As a valued new customer, we would appreciate you taking the time to answer the following questions:

- Did your cleaner arrive on time? Yes
- Did they spend the agreed amount of time at your premises? Yes
- Were you satisfied with the standard of cleaning? Yes
- If not, why not?
- Will you be using the service again? Yes

For our records, please supply the following information:

Name:

Company:

Telephone:

e-mail:

Thank you for taking the time to complete the questionnaire. Please return it in the enclosed prepaid envelope.

Customer Satisfaction Questionnaire - Sparkle Cleaning Services

You have recently used Sparkle Cleaning Services for the first time.

As a valued new customer, we would appreciate you taking the time to answer the following questions:

- Did your cleaner arrive on time? No
- Did they spend the agreed amount of time at your premises? Yes
- Were you satisfied with the standard of cleaning? No
- If not, why not? He left dirty water in one of the sinks and the ladies' toilet was not cleaned thoroughly.
- Will you be using the service again? Don't know

Comment: Interview the cleaner about these comments

For our records, please supply the following information:

Name: Mona Lott

Company: Thickett and Pratt Solicitors

Telephone: 0123 456789

e-mail: mona_l@somewhere.net

Thank you for taking the time to complete the questionnaire. Please return it in the enclosed prepaid envelope.

Answers

Exercise 38

Sample solutions for this exercise are saved as **Locations Edit Solution**, **Feedback Edit Solution**, **Smalltown Solution** and **Buyers Info Solution** (**Smalltown Solution** and **Buyers Info Solution** not shown below) in the **Word Processing Solutions** folder.

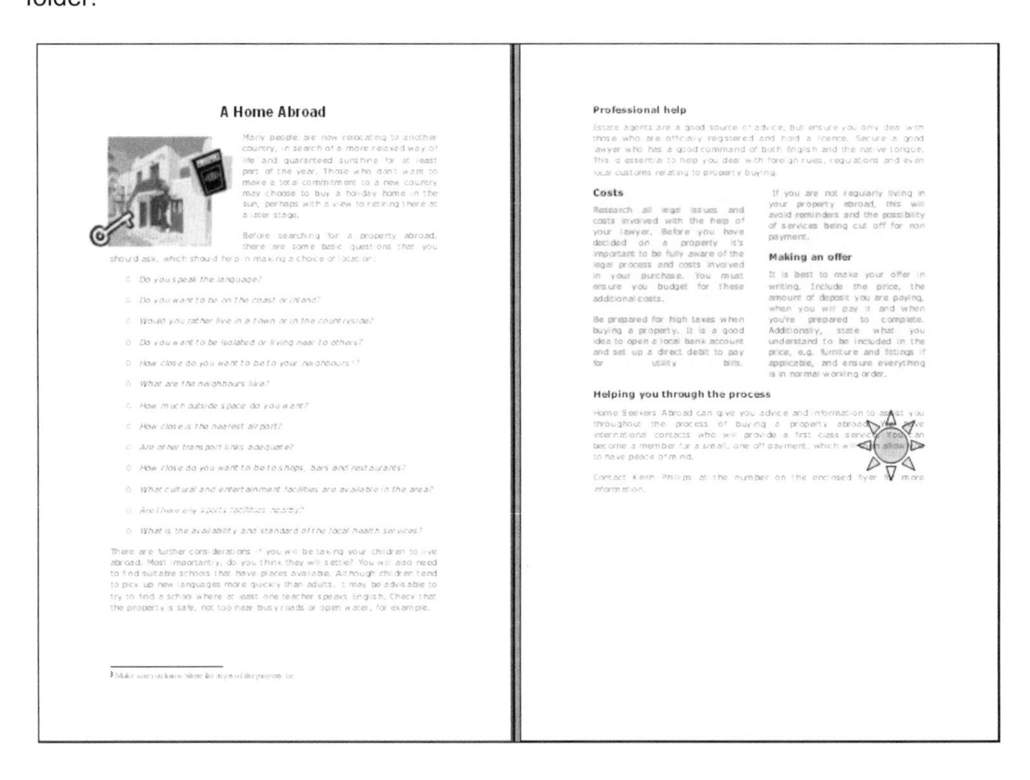

A Home Abroad

Many people are now relocating to another country, in search of a more relaxed way of life and guaranteed sunshine for at least part of the year. Those who don't want to make a total commitment to a new country may choose to buy a holiday home in the sun, perhaps with a view to retiring there at a later stage.

Before searching for a property abroad, there are some basic questions that you should ask, which should help in making a choice of location:

- *Do you speak the language?*
- *Do you want to be on the coast or inland?*
- *Would you rather live in a town or in the countryside?*
- *Do you want to be isolated or living near to others?*
- *How close do you want to be to your neighbours*[3]*?*
- *What are the neighbours like?*
- *How much outside space do you want?*
- *How close is the nearest airport?*
- *Are other transport links adequate?*
- *How close do you want to be to shops, bars and restaurants?*
- *What cultural and entertainment facilities are available in the area?*
- *Are there any sports facilities nearby?*
- *What is the availability and standard of the local health services?*

There are further considerations if you will be taking your children to live abroad. Most importantly, do you think they will settle? You will also need to find suitable schools that have places available. Although children tend to pick up new languages more quickly than adults, it may be advisable to try to find a school where at least one teacher speaks English. Check that the property is safe, not too near busy roads or open water, for example.

3 [illegible]

Professional help

Estate agents are a good source of advice, but ensure you only deal with those who are officially registered and hold a licence. Secure a good lawyer who has a good command of both English and the native tongue. This is essential to help you deal with foreign rules, regulations and even local customs relating to property buying.

Costs

Research all legal issues and costs involved with the help of your lawyer. Before you have decided on a property it's important to be fully aware of the legal process and costs involved in your purchase. You must ensure you budget for these additional costs.

Be prepared for high taxes when buying a property. It is a good idea to open a local bank account and set up a direct debit to pay for utility bills. If you are not regularly living in your property abroad, this will avoid reminders and the possibility of services being cut off for non payment.

Making an offer

It is best to make your offer in writing. Include the price, the amount of deposit you are paying, when you will pay it and when you're prepared to complete. Additionally, state what you understand to be included in the price, e.g. furniture and fittings if applicable, and ensure everything is in normal working order.

Helping you through the process

Home Seekers Abroad can give you advice and information to assist you throughout the process of buying a property abroad. We have international contacts who will provide a first class service. You can become a member for a small, one off payment, which will then allow you to have peace of mind.

Contact Keith Phillips at the number on the enclosed flyer for more information.

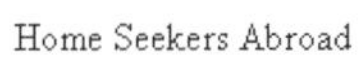

Home Seekers Abroad
To help us with market research, please take a few moments
to answer the following questions:
Where did you hear about the company? Internet search
What type of property are you looking to buy? House or villa
Do you want a property with a pool? Yes
Does the property have to be detached? Yes
Are you looking near the coast or inland? Inland
Do you want a rural or urban property? Rural
Are you prepared to renovate? Yes
Please supply your e-mail address
Thank you for taking the time to complete his questionnaire.
Please indicate if you would like us to e-mail you our monthly newsletter by checking the box.

Other Products from CiA Training

If you have enjoyed using this guide you can obtain other products from our range of over 150 titles. CiA Training Ltd is a leader in developing self-teach training materials and courseware.

Open Learning Guides

Teach yourself by working through them in your own time. Our range includes products for: Windows, Word, Excel, Access, PowerPoint, Project, Publisher, Internet Explorer, FrontPage and many more… We also have a large back catalogue of products; please call for details.

ECDL/ICDL

We produce accredited training materials for the European Computer Driving Licence (ECDL/ICDL) and the Advanced ECDL/ICDL qualifications. The standard level consists of seven modules and the advanced level four modules. Material produced covers a variety of Microsoft Office products from Office 97 to 2003.

e-Citizen

Courseware for this exciting new qualification is available now. Students will become proficient Internet users and participate confidently in all major aspects of the online world with the expert guidance of this handbook. Simulated web sites are also supplied for safe practice before tackling the real thing.

New CLAiT, CLAiT Plus and CLAiT Advanced

Open learning publications are now available for the new OCR CLAiT 2006 qualifications. The publications enable the user to learn the features needed to pass the assessments using a gradual step by step approach.

Trainer's Packs

Specifically written for use with tutor led I.T. courses. The trainer is supplied with a trainer guide (step by step exercises), course notes (for delegates), consolidation exercises (for use as reinforcement) and course documents (course contents, pre-course questionnaires, evaluation forms, certificate template, etc). All supplied on CD with rights to edit and copy the documents.

Online Shop

To purchase or browse the CiA catalogue please visit, *www.ciatraining.co.uk*.